Vocal Music
of the Revolutionary and Federal Era

The
WESTERN WIND
American Tune-Book

Edited by
Lawrence Bennett

Introductory Notes by
Lawrence Bennett and Steven Urkowitz

BROUDE BROTHERS LIMITED
New York

Library of Congress Catalogue Card Number: 76-062983

ISBN 0-8450-0076-4

© Copyright 1974, 1975, 1976 by Broude Brothers Limited

For
Irving Lowens,
Friend of American Music

Acknowledgments

One of the chief pleasures experienced by the editors during the preparation of the present collection was the opportunity to work with many performers, scholars, librarians, and friends of American music. All were extremely generous and helpful.

The editors are especially indebted to the five other members of the Western Wind. From William Zukof came much of the inspiration and the original idea for the anthology. William Lyon Lee prepared most of the music manuscripts and gave countless fruitful suggestions throughout the editorial process. Janet Steele assisted with the organization and editing of the final manuscript and provided the keyboard realization for Holden's *Ode on Music*. Janet Sullivan and Elliot Levine helped with numerous technical and editorial matters. The group as a whole spent many hours selecting music and reading proofs. In addition, the editors would like to thank Nancy Bennett, who typed many of the texts and offered consistently practical advice, and Susan Urkowitz, whose insights illuminated the text interpretations presented before each group of pieces.

Scholars of American music proved to be unusually helpful and sympathetic. Paul C. Echols gave timely encouragement to the project during its initial stages. Irving Lowens generously directed the Western Wind's attention to a number of tune-books which contain remarkably rich repertory. The editors are particularly grateful to Richard Crawford, who supplied lists of concordances as well as numerous biographical and historical details. For information concerning the origins of the folk-tunes and texts of the compositions by Jeremiah Ingalls, the editors are indebted to David Klocko. Sterling Murray offered many useful suggestions with regard to performance practices. The editors would also like to thank Barbara Petersen, our helpful and patient editor at Broude Brothers, as well as David P. McKay, Betty Bandel, and Geoffrey Weston.

Among the many librarians who assisted the editors, Diana Haskell of the Newberry Library and Jon Newsom of the Music Division at the Library of Congress deserve a special word of thanks. The editors also appreciate the efforts of the staffs of the Rare Book Room and the Music Division of the New York Public Library, where much of our research was carried out.

The Western Wind

Janet Steele, soprano
Janet Sullivan, soprano
William Zukof, countertenor
Steven Urkowitz, dramatic supervisor

Lawrence Bennett, tenor
William Lyon Lee, tenor
Elliot Levine, baritone

The Western Wind was formed by a group of singers who enjoy making music together. Since 1969 the ensemble has been exploring great vocal music from the Middle Ages to the twentieth century. In 1973 their recording of *Early American Vocal Music* (Nonesuch H-71276) was nominated for a Grammy Award and was named Record of the Year by *Stereo Review*. Their Library of Congress performance of "Music in the New World," taped by the Voice of America, was broadcast world-wide on July 4, 1976. The ensemble was also seen on a PBS special, *Amazing Grace,* a ninety-minute program of American music.

In 1974 the Western Wind's second recording, Orazio Vecchi's *L'Amfiparnaso* (Nonesuch H-71286), was called "a virtuoso achievement" by *Opera News* and was chosen Best Record of the Month by *Stereo Review*. Since their summer in residence at Dartmouth College in 1975, the Western Wind has given concerts and workshops from Maine to California. Works have been written especially for the group by composers such as William Bolcom, John Graziano, Tzipora Jochsberger, Charlie Morrow, Peter Perrin, and Andy Thomas. Represented by Colbert Artists Management, the Western Wind is available for concerts, workshops, and open reading sessions.

Table of Contents

TABLE OF CONTENTS

Introduction

The Western Wind American Tune-Book is intended for the pleasure of singers. With the publication of this collection, the Western Wind would like to share the experience of part-singing with all who enjoy music—seasoned performers, amateur musicians, and dedicated listeners. For those social singers already familiar with the joys of Medieval, Renaissance, and other part-songs, this book serves as an introduction to a little known but extravagantly rich repertory which flowered during the early years of our nation. Written by the masters of singing-schools, where young and old learned to read music and to take pleasure in part-singing, the compositions presented here afford ample testimony to the originality, emotional intensity, and communal spirit of early American music.

The pieces selected for this collection were composed during the Revolutionary and Federal periods of United States history (roughly 1775 to 1820). But behind this repertory there stands a century and a half of tradition, for ever since the first colonies had been settled, music-making had been an important aspect of American life. The earliest settlers brought with them books of psalm and hymn texts. Indeed, the first book of any kind printed in New England was such a collection, *The Bay Psalm Book* (1640). The melodies associated with these texts were preserved not by printing but by oral tradition. Throughout the seventeenth and early eighteenth centuries, Americans continued to sing the familiar hymn tunes from memory. Bit by bit, however, the original melodies underwent changes as each new generation of singers, by accident or design, re-created the music which had been handed down to it. By 1720 so much individual and local variation in the performance of traditional melodies existed that a group of clergymen instituted singing-schools in order to eliminate what some considered "an horrid Medley of confused and disorderly Noises"[1] that prevailed in New England churches.

Originally intended to provide instruction in psalm-singing and in the rudiments of reading musical notation, singing-schools soon became the commercial enterprises of individuals. Typically, an itinerant singing-master would come into a town and advertise his offering of a three-month course to be given at a specific location—often a church or school, but sometimes a tavern or meeting-house. Persons of all ages and social classes would enroll, frequently by signing a formal agreement or charter pledging themselves to rules of prompt attendance and decorous behavior and to the payment of fees. From many diaries and letters, we learn that the schools were particularly popular with young people who found that when crowded together in the cause of learning they might also involve themselves in surreptitious flirtation. In

---

[1] Thomas Walter, *The Grounds and Rules of Musick Explained: Or, An Introduction to the Art of Singing by Note* (Boston, 1721), p. 2. For a discussion of the controversy on the uniformity of psalm singing, see Gilbert Chase, *America's Music* (New York, 1955), pp. 22–40.

INTRODUCTION

1782, one young man complained to a fellow student:

> . . . I have no Inclination for anything for I am almost sick of the
> World & were it not for the Hopes of going to singing-meeting tonight
> & indulging myself a little in some of the carnal Delights of the Flesh,
> such as kissing, squeezing &c. &c., I should willingly leave it now,
> before 10 o'clock & exchange it for a better.[2]

For nearly fifty years singing-masters drew chiefly upon contemporary English compilations for examples of harmonized psalm- and hymn-tunes. By the 1770s, when English imports of all sorts were being rejected in favor of colonial products, American musicians were beginning to publish tune-books which included many of their own compositions. And by 1810, when the demand for music by local tunesmiths had begun to subside—at least in New England—thousands of compositions had been published in more than three hundred tune-books.

The largely self-taught New England composers who pioneered our earliest music were usually tradesmen who supplemented their incomes by publishing tune-books and by conducting singing-schools. William Billings, for example, was a tanner, Jeremiah Ingalls a cooper, Justin Morgan a teacher and horse breeder, and Daniel Read a general storekeeper and comb manufacturer. Often working in relative isolation and in most cases unfettered by European tradition, these men produced music that was uniquely American—rough-hewn and adapted to the social needs of their age.

The hallmark of the New England singing-school style is its emphasis on strong melodic writing in each of the parts. Since the composers knew that each singer derived his greatest pleasure from "holding" a good tune against several others, they sought to provide each part with a maximum of melodic interest. The harmonies that resulted were often unorthodox by European standards. The pieces collected here offer an abundance of open-fifth cadences, sets of parallel fifths and octaves, unusual doublings, striking dissonances, and direct cross relations. The melodic inventiveness and harmonic boldness of these compositions account in large part for their unusual freshness and appeal to modern ears.

The texts which the composers of the New England singing-school tradition chose to set were almost exclusively religious ones. (We do, however, find a few settings of patriotic poems written in connection with specific occasions such as the Battle of Bunker Hill or the birthday of George Washington.) These texts represent the truly popular poetry of the eighteenth century in both England and America. It must be remembered that the eighteenth century was an era of great diversity: the Age of Reason was also the time of the First Great Awakening, the earliest of several waves of religious fervor which swept across America and even reached back over the Atlantic to England. Within this poetic and social context, composers were able to select texts dealing with the entire range of human experience: we encounter among the texts which were set celebrations of erotic passions, dramatic narratives of Biblical events, and personal meditations on the subjects of joy, despair, grief, death, and the nature of religious faith. The main sources for these texts were compilations of metrical psalm translations and devotional poetry. Among the most widely used of such anthologies were those assembled by Isaac Watts, the Wesleys, and Tate and Brady. These enormously popular

---

[2] Cited by Irving Lowens, *Music and Musicians in Early America* (New York, 1964), p. 282.

collections went through hundreds of English and American editions. Individual copies were so heavily used that many of the volumes preserved in libraries today have actually been read to tatters.

Not all of the pieces presented here were written by native-born composers of the New England singing-school tradition. In the late eighteenth century, a number of European-trained composers emigrated to America. Prominent among such "new Americans" were the English organist William Selby and the Danish musician Hans Gram. Selby, who left a promising career in London to come to Boston, was thoroughly versed in traditional harmony. He was active not only as a composer of instrumental and vocal music, but also as a performer and teacher. Gram appears to have exerted considerable influence upon singing-masters such as Oliver Holden and Samuel Holyoke, who collaborated with him in bringing out *The Massachusetts Compiler* (Boston, 1795). Both Holden and Holyoke seem to have been among the first American composers to have had training in harmony, and it may well be that they owed much of their musical knowledge—and taste—to Gram.

Toward the end of the eighteenth century, several leading American-born singing-masters began actively to advocate the adoption of traditional European musical style. Men like Holden, Holyoke, and Andrew Law included numerous pieces by European composers in their own published collections. They repeatedly proclaimed the superiority of so-called "scientific music," while crying down works composed in the native style. Their attitude is reflected by remarks such as Holden's lament that "among *so many* American authors *so little* can be found well written, or well adapted to sacred purposes."[3]

Nevertheless, the American singing-school tradition enjoyed the support of many composers well into the nineteenth century. Writing to Andrew Law in 1811, Elkanah Kelsay Dare defended the efforts of his fellow Americans:

> I freely acquiesce with you that the European teachers & authors . . . have had a longer experience than we have—but that *their* composition only is elegant & suitable for divine worship I cannot admit. We can claim a Billings, a Morgan, a Swan, a Hall &c., which claim no small share of merit.[4]

The shortcoming of American music, Dare felt, was not composition, but performance, and he took to task the same sort of slovenly congregational singing which the eighteenth-century singing-masters had attempted to cure:

> What destroys the beauty & solemnity of sacred music, in my opinion, more than the mere composition, is the rough & erroneous manner in which it is taught. *Piano & forte, lively, moderate,* &c., are roughly hurried over in the same monotony of sound. Singing mournful & pensive psalms on the major key, and as fast as the tongue can pronounce the Words, & sometimes faster. This does more real injury than instances of bad composition.[5]

Dare's response was that of a Delaware man writing at a time when the

---

[3] Preface to *The Worcester Collection,* eighth edition (Boston, 1803).

[4] A transcription of passages from Dare's letter to Law, dated 25 June 1811, appears in Richard Crawford's *Andrew Law, American Psalmodist* (Evanston, 1968), pp. 210–12. The original manuscript of Dare's letter is to be found in the Andrew Law Papers (L 134) in the William L. Clements Library at the University of Michigan, Ann Arbor.

[5] *Ibid.*

INTRODUCTION

center of the singing-school tradition was shifting away from the populous, fashion-conscious cities along the East Coast where the European style was eventually to triumph. Although on the wane in New England, the singing-school tradition did not disappear: in keeping with its pioneer nature, it moved inland to what in the early nineteenth century was the American South and West. There it flourished in Virginia, Kentucky, Tennessee, Ohio, and the Mississippi Valley.

Publication of new tune-books in the South and West was stimulated by the early nineteenth-century religious movement known as the Second Great Awakening. The chief occasions for singing both new and familiar tunes were the revivalist camp meetings, outdoor religious gatherings which provided for their participants an intensely emotional religious experience. To the faithful pilgrims who sometimes traveled hundreds of miles to attend them, such meetings provided both social nourishment and spiritual renewal.

For these meetings and for the long pilgrimages, editors of tune-books published a vast repertory of song. This repertory included anthems such as Billings' *I Am the Rose of Sharon*, plain-tunes such as Morgan's *Amanda*, and fuging-tunes such as Ingalls' *Northfield*, works which had enjoyed great popularity in the North. While Southern composers continued to write in some of the familiar New England forms, the folk-hymn soon emerged as the musical genre most characteristic of the Second Great Awakening. Although an oral tradition of combining a secular folk-tune with a religious text had probably existed in New England as early as the 1730s, the first printed folk-hymns began to appear almost simultaneously with the rise of camp meetings in the opening years of the nineteenth century. To the growing body of folk-hymns, Southern compilers added a related repertory of religious ballads and revival spiritual songs.[6] The tuneful, folkish quality of the music and the rough, colloquial language of many of the texts were well suited to rural, frontier religious experience.

During the early years of the Second Great Awakening, the folk-hymn appears to have been transmitted from New England to the Southern tradition by way of western Pennsylvania. The present collection includes pieces which were first published in Pennsylvania and which were to be frequently performed and widely reprinted in the South and West. The major musical collection inspired by the beginning of the Second Great Awakening is John Wyeth's *Repository of Sacred Music, Part Second,* published in Harrisburg, Pennsylvania in 1813. Probably not an active musician himself, Wyeth (1770–1858) nevertheless holds an important position in the history of American music as the editor and publisher of two remarkable collections of sacred vocal music, the *Repository of Sacred Music* (Harrisburg, 1810)[7] and *Part Second*. Unlike its predecessor, *Part Second* was not merely a collection of previously published tunes; rather, it contained more than fifty pieces that had never before appeared in print—among them numerous folk-hymns, religious ballads, and revival spiritual songs.

Although Southern compilers frequently drew upon standard eighteenth-century collections of hymn texts, they also turned to the work of more recent

[6] For a discussion of these three genres, see George Pullen Jackson, *Spiritual Folk-Songs of Early America* (Locust Valley, N.Y., 1937), pp. 4–9.

[7] According to Irving Lowens, the *Repository of Sacred Music* enjoyed extraordinary success, selling approximately 125,000 copies at a time when the entire American population was less than seven million.

INTRODUCTION

poets—both English and American—and to folk-derived material. Many anonymous revivalist poems were published for the first time in the tune-books themselves.

Even after the 1840s, when the fervor of the Second Great Awakening had declined, the singing-school tradition survived in parts of the South and West. In New England, the birthplace of the singing-school, however, the growing preference for the European style meant that the music of Billings and his fellow tunesmiths would be first neglected and then forgotten. Only during the last thirty years has a resurgence of interest in the music of the singing-masters enabled us to see their work as a unique flowering of American art. In this volume we have attempted to outline the history of the tradition, to capture the essence of the music, and to explain the significance of the texts. But there is no better way to understand and to appreciate this repertory than to sing it. We leave it now to singers to bring the music in this collection to life.

SUGGESTIONS FOR PERFORMANCE

For indications of how the music was performed, we may turn to the tune-books themselves. While the practices they reflect vary with the date and place of publication, certain general rules may be extracted and applied—with care—by modern performers. These general rules are qualified or supplemented by specific comments about the individual pieces. The aspects most frequently considered include tempo, special practices with regard to voicings and doublings, the application of ornamentation, and the use of instruments.

Tempo

The tune-books provide few specific tempo markings. However, many singing-masters evidently observed a close relationship between tempo and time signature. Thus William Billings indicates proper tempi for the nine common time signatures or "moods of time," and from his instructions, we can devise the following table:

Time Signature	Metronome Equivalent
C (the "Adagio" mood)	♩ = 60
₵ (the "Largo" mood)	♩ = 80
⊅ (the "Allegro" mood)	♩ = 60
2/4	♩ = 120
3/2	♩ = 60
3/4	♩ = 80
3/8	♩. = 53
6/4	♩ = 80 or 60
6/8	♩. = 80

SUGGESTIONS FOR PERFORMANCE

On the other hand, E. K. Dare, while concurring with Billings on many tempi, differs on certain important ones:

Time Signature	Metronome Equivalent
C	♩ = 60
¢	♩ = 80
⊅	♩ = 60
2/4	♩ = 120
3/2	♩ = 60
3/4	♩ = 120
3/8	♪ = 120
6/4	♩. = 60
6/8	♩. = 120

The tempi recommended in *The Western Wind American Tune-Book* do not always conform to the "rules" given in the theoretical introductions. Following the advice of several late eighteenth-century singing-masters that textual and stylistic considerations should not be outweighed by absolute metronomic markings, the editor has often suggested tempi slightly quicker or slower for modern performance.

Voicings and doublings

The anthems and other large compositions published in the present collection can be performed successfully by a chorus or by a chamber ensemble. The shorter pieces (plain-tunes, fuging-tunes, folk-hymns, and patriotic odes) can be sung by a large group, a chamber ensemble, or soloists. The principal tune—in the top voice of the two-part pieces, in the middle voice of the three-part compositions, and in the tenor line of the four-part works—should always be prominent. Many singing-masters, including Billings, strongly urge the addition of extra male voices to the bottom line "because the Bass is the Foundation, and Therefore in order to have good Music, there must be Three Bass to one of the upper parts. . . ."[8]

In the four-part pieces, the tenor may be doubled an octave above by a few sopranos, and the soprano part may be reinforced an octave below by some tenors if the performing group is large enough. The result will be a rich six-part texture characteristic of the eighteenth-century singing-school style. If this doubling is used, a similar procedure can be adopted for the remaining voices. In the plain-tunes, the tune may be sung by sopranos only and the top part by tenors only, a practice recommended by several singing-masters. Octave doublings may also be effective in the two- and three-part compositions.

Present-day performers may find it desirable to experiment with a variety of sonorities. Most eighteenth- and early nineteenth-century publications do not specify what voices are to sing which lines. It appears that many pieces were sung by whatever combination was available at the moment. The Western Wind has found that many of the shorter two- and three-part pieces are

---

[8] William Billings, *The New England Psalm-Singer* (Boston, 1770), p. 18.

particularly suitable for men's voices, while others are effective when sung by women's voices, the altos transposing the bass part up an octave.

Ornamentation

For modern performance, the addition of some vocal ornamentation would also be consistent with the style. In the theoretical introductions to many tune-books, compilers describe a variety of embellishments. However, the only ornaments which appear to have been widely used were the trill ("shake") and the passing tone ("grace of transition"). Occasionally, as in the anthem *Hamshire* and in the patriotic odes, trills were indicated by the composers. More often, however, they were applied during performance by the singers. As in contemporary European practice, trills customarily began on the pitch above the notated pitch. For less experienced singers, several singing-masters suggest the substitution of an inverted mordent or a turn for a trill. Passing tones were frequently used to fill in the interval of a third or a fourth.

Present-day performers may find it desirable to ornament many of the compositions included in *The Western Wind American Tune-Book*. The editor particularly recommends the addition of embellishments for repeated sections, notably in the fuging-tunes and in the anthem *I Am the Rose of Sharon*.

The use of instruments

During most of the eighteenth century, a cappella singing appears to have been the norm. Although frequently resisted by pious religious denominations, organs were nevertheless installed in a few large New England churches during the eighteenth century and became increasingly common after 1800. Other instruments appear to have been used to accompany singers in meeting-houses from about 1760 and in churches after 1790. The most common instruments used were the "bass viol" (which actually more closely resembled the modern-day violoncello than the viola da gamba), members of the violin family, flute, clarinet, and bassoon. After 1800, groups of such instruments—the so-called "gallery orchestras"—were widely used in rural New England.

Of the pieces presented in *The Western Wind American Tune-Book,* only the anthem *Hamshire* includes original instrumental passages—two-part "Symphonies" for unspecified instruments. The use of organ or harpsichord continuo in pieces such as the patriotic odes and Holden's *Ode on Music* seems appropriate in view of the composer's knowledge of traditional harmony. Elsewhere, discreet doubling by organ or by melodic instruments such as flute, clarinet, violin, cello, or double bass can be effective. For the folk-hymns, performers may also wish to experiment with instrumental obbligatos such as the one provided by Stuart Schulman for *Fiducia.*

EDITORIAL POLICY

The editions of the 51 pieces printed in the present collection are based upon American sources dating from 1775 to 1820. In each case the editor has chosen a principal source—sometimes the first publication or sometimes the earliest print in which its composer is known to have had a hand. In several cases the editor has elected to base his edition on *Wyeth's Repository, Part Second,* because the versions found in this collection became the models for tune-books of the Southern tradition. In preparing the texts, the editor has followed the readings found in the tune-books themselves, even when these depart from authoritative editions of the poetry: the editions thus printed probably reflect what was sung. Capitalization, punctuation, and spelling have been made consistent with modern usage.

In the present edition, the original tempo and dynamic markings have been printed in roman type. All editorial additions are given in italics. The editor has substituted modern clefs and time signatures for the original symbols. Several pieces have been rebarred or provided with alternative barring in order to clarify the intended irregular rhythmic groupings. The editor has also indicated the tune in the homophonic sections of the three- and four-part pieces and has added keyboard reductions for all compositions having more than two parts.

The first page of Oliver Holden's *Ode on Music* as it was printed in *American Harmony* (Boston, 1792), reduced to 75%.

Ode on Music

"Great art thou O MUSIC! and with thee there is no competitor," exclaimed
William Billings in the preface to *The Singing-Master's Assistant* (Boston, 1778),
p. 31. Billings' enthusiasm for the art of music was certainly shared by Oliver
Holden and the host of other singing-masters who provided early America
with a vast repertory of song for social entertainment and religious devotion.
In his first published collection, *American Harmony* (Boston, 1792), Holden
included two pieces entitled *Ode on Music,* one of which is presented here.

About the text and music

The text of *Ode on Music* is taken from the opening lines of Alexander
Pope's "Ode for Music on Saint Cecilia's Day" (1713), written in honor of
the patron saint of musicians. The text opens with an invocation of the Muses
("ye Nine"), the daughters of Zeus who preside over the arts and sciences:
they are asked to descend to earth, there to inspire a concert of voices and
instruments. The text then indicates the range of effects of which music
thus inspired may be capable, thereby giving the composer the opportunity
to illustrate through his music the words which the singers sing. Note, for
example, the half and whole notes with which "While, in more lengthened
notes" is set in measures 57 ff., and the ascending lines, first *forte* and then
fortissimo, to which "louder and louder and yet louder rise" are sung in measures
83 ff.

For performance

The tempo and dynamic indications given in *American Harmony* are here
printed in roman type; all editorial additions are printed in italics. The editor
has suggested a tempo somewhat faster than the "rule" recommended by
most singing-masters that in 3/2 $\downarrow$ = 60. *Ode on Music* can be performed
by soloists or by chorus. (If a large ensemble is used, measures 23–35 should
still be sung by a soprano soloist, as indicated in the original source.) The
tune, which is in the middle voice of the three-part sections, should always
be prominent. *Ode on Music* is a piece which the Western Wind has found
to be particularly effective when sung by soprano, tenor, and bass. Alternatively,
some performers may prefer two voice parts of the same range (either sopranos
or tenors) above the bass line. If so, the usual octave doublings can be employed.
The realization of the continuo part which accompanies the soprano solo
has been provided by Janet Steele; it can be played by either harpsichord
or organ, which can also double the vocal lines in the three-part sections.
The individual parts might also be doubled by melodic instruments such
as violin, clarinet, violoncello, or double bass.

On the sources

The present edition of *Ode on Music* is based upon the version found in
the *American Harmony*. The three *errata* cited by Holden in the introduction
to this source have been corrected in the present edition.

1
ODE ON MUSIC

For Mixed Voices (STB), Soprano Solo, and Continuo

Alexander Pope
(1688-1744)

OLIVER HOLDEN
(1765-1844)

Treble solo
Moderato (♩ = c. 84)

Soprano

In a sad-ly pleas-ing strain, Let the war - bling flute ___ com-plain, Let the war - bling flute com - plain, Let the war - bling flute com - plain.

Continuo*

tr

* Continuo realization by Janet Steele

13

14

18

Seven Fuging-Tunes

The typical American fuging-tune, a form which was popular in New England from ca. 1770 to 1810, is a short musical setting of a metrical psalm or hymn text. Its form is *ABB*. The *A* section consists of a brief homophonic statement which arrives at either a full or a half cadence. The *B* section begins with a point of imitation taken up by each voice in turn (the "fuge") and concludes with a short chordal passage. The entire *B* section is then repeated. Irving Lowens has demonstrated that the origins of the fuging-tune lie not in the fugues of the Baroque masters, as has often been assumed, but rather in "fuging," the English Renaissance practice of imitative writing, both strict and free.[1]

About the texts and music

Jeremiah Ingalls' *Northfield* was first published in the fifth edition of *The Village Harmony* (Exeter, N.H., 1800) and by 1808 had appeared in at least twelve collections. *Northfield*'s text comes from Isaac Watts's *Hymns and Spiritual Songs* (London, 1707): it is an appeal to the Messiah to hasten "the welcome day" of his second coming. The *A* section consists of a vigorous question, "How long, dear Savior . . . ?" while the *B* section is an urgent prayer for action, "Fly swifter round. . . ."

The anonymous *Canaan* was first printed in the second edition of *Wyeth's Repository of Sacred Music, Part Second* (Harrisburg, 1820). The text, taken from *Hymns Founded on Various Texts in the Holy Scriptures, By the Late Philip Doddridge, D.D.* (London, 1755), follows one of the various patterns of formal meditations. The first stanza is intended as a preparation for a religious experience ("Unite, my roving thoughts . . . "), the second stanza reports a manifestation of the Divine Presence in the world ("Jehovah's awful voice is heard . . ."), and the third stanza recounts the effects of Jehovah's presence (". . . the tempest . . . subsides . . ."). The meditative experience calls forth a vow to reform ("I charge my heart . . . to give its follies o'er").

The anonymous *Lonsdale*, like *Canaan*, was first printed in the second edition of *Wyeth's Repository, Part Second*. Its text, taken from Watts's *Hymns and Spiritual Songs*, proceeds from the premise, stated in the *A* section, that "a thousand sacred sweets" are available to enrich the holy life spent climbing the "Hill of Zion" to the New Jerusalem. The *B* section, which recommends singing as one of the sacred pleasures, calls for an end to weeping over earthly sorrows. The piece concludes with the reminder that in the sanctified life we are ". . . marching to Immanuel's ground, to fairer worlds on high."

Oliver Holden's *New Canaan* was the most popular of the seven fuging-tunes presented here. First printed in the anonymous collection *The Federal Harmony* (Boston, 1788), *New Canaan* had by 1801 appeared in no fewer than eighteen tune-books. The text of *New Canaan* is taken from the Ninety-third Psalm

---

[1] Irving Lowens, "The Origins of the American Fuging-Tune," *Journal of the American Musicological Society*, VI (1953), 46–47.

in Watts's *The Psalms of David Imitated in the Language of the New Testament* (London, 1719); it proudly celebrates the immutability of the Lord's sovereignty over a universe subject to assaults by both men and nature.

J. West's *Windsor* was first published in Elisha West's *The Musical Concert* (Northampton, 1802). The anonymous text offers another image of God's presence, which extends even beyond Judgment Day, "when rolling years shall cease to move."

Stephen Jenks's *Decay* seems to have appeared only in the composer's own collection, *The Delights of Harmony* (Dedham, Mass., 1805). The anonymous text is a simple but dramatic reminder that "life may end in an hour."

Elisha West's *Evening Hymn*, like *Windsor*, was first published in *The Musical Concert*. In this source, the music was printed with Watts's text "Our moments fly apace." The text given in the present edition first appeared with West's music in Ingalls' *The Christian Harmony* (Exeter, N.H., 1805): it is attributed to John Leland (1754–1801), and was first printed in the eighth edition of Joshua Smith's *Divine Hymns, or Spiritual Songs* (Exeter, N.H., 1801). The words evoke that consciousness of death which makes mankind at once both prudent and heroic: if "we all remember well" our approaching death, we can make each day precious and each accomplishment urgent.

For performance

None of the sources gives indications of tempo, dynamics, or ornamentation. For five of the fuging-tunes printed here, the editor has suggested tempi that depart from the "rule" given by most singing-masters that in cut time $\downarrow$ = 60. It should be noted that in *Canaan, New Canaan,* and *Evening Hymn* the dynamics suggested by the editor are applicable only to the texts of the first stanzas. In *Lonsdale,* the editor has scored the upper parts (which the source gives in the treble clef) for tenors. However, both tenor parts may be sung by sopranos instead of tenors (as called for in the source), or tenors may be doubled by sopranos. All of the fuging-tunes can be performed by a large chorus, a chamber ensemble, or soloists.

On the sources

The present editions of *Northfield* and *Evening Hymn* are based upon the versions printed by Ingalls in *The Christian Harmony*. *Lonsdale* and *Canaan* are based upon the second edition of *Wyeth's Repository, Part Second*. *New Canaan* is printed from the version issued by Holden in the first volume of his collection *The Union Harmony* (Boston, 1793), the earliest source for this piece in which the composer is known to have had a hand. The editions of *Windsor* and *Decay* are based on their initial printings. In both *Canaan* and *New Canaan,* stanzas 2 through 4 do not appear in the tune-books upon which the editions are based. These stanzas are taken from the original Doddridge and Watts publications.

2
NORTHFIELD
For Mixed Voices (SATB) a cappella

Isaac Watts
(1674-1748)

JEREMIAH INGALLS
(1764-1838)

Vigorously ($\d$ = c. 84)

Soprano *and Tenor*
How long, dear Sav - ior, O how long Shall

Alto
How long, dear Sav - ior, O how long Shall

Tenor *and Soprano*
TUNE
How long, dear Sav - ior, O how long Shall

Bass
How long, dear Sav - ior, O how long Shall

Vigorously ($\d$ = c. 84)

Keyboard *for rehearsal only*

this bright hour de - lay?   *f (p 2nd time)*

this bright hour de - lay?   *f (p 2nd time)*   Fly

this bright hour de - lay?   *f (p 2nd time)*   Fly swift - er round the

this bright hour de - lay?   Fly swift - er round the wheel of time,* Fly

f (p 2nd time)

* Editions of the text read:"Fly swifter round, ye wheels of time ....".

21

22

3

CANAAN

For Mixed Voices (SATB) a cappella

Philip Doddridge
(1702-1751)

Anonymous

3. Harmonious accents to my soul
   The sounds of peace convey;
   The tempest at his word subsides,
   And winds and seas obey.

4. By all its joys, I charge my heart
   To grieve his love no more;
   But, charm'd by melody divine,
   To give its follies o'er.

4
LONSDALE

For TTB and/or SSB a cappella

Isaac Watts
(1674-1748)

Anonymous

* If sopranos are used instead of tenors, the right hand should be played an octave higher.

26

5
NEW CANAAN
For Mixed Voices (SATB) a cappella

Isaac Watts
(1674-1748)

OLIVER HOLDEN
(1765-1844)

maj - es - ty a - round. round.
ev - er stands on high. high.

2. Upheld by thy commands,
   The world securely stands,
   And skies and stars obey the word.
   Thy throne was fix'd on high
   Ere stars adorn'd the sky:
   Eternal is thy kingdom, Lord.

3. In vain the noisy crowd,
   Like billows fierce and loud,
   Against thine empire rage and roar;
   In vain, with angry spite,
   The surly nations fight
   And dash like waves against the shore.

5. Thy promises are true;
   Thy grace is ever new:
   There fix'd, thy church shall ne'er remove.
   Thy saints, with holy fear,
   Shall in thy courts appear
   And sing thine everlasting love.

6
WINDSOR

For Mixed Voices (SATB) a cappella

Anonymous

J. WEST
(fl. c. 1790)

* Original: g'- a'

7
DECAY
For Mixed Voices (SATB) a cappella

Anonymous

STEPHEN JENKS
(1772-1856)

8

EVENING HYMN

For Mixed Voices (SATB) a cappella

John Leland
(1754-1841)

ELISHA WEST
(1756 - after 1808)

3. Lord, keep us safe this night,
   Secure from all our fears;
   May angels guard us while we sleep,
   Till morning light appears.

4. And when we early rise
   And view th' unwearied sun,
   May we set out to win the prize
   And after glory run.

5. And when our days are past
   And we from time remove,
   O may we in thy bosom rest,
   The bosom of thy love.

Three Anthems from The Song of Solomon

William Billings, probably the best known of all early American composers, wrote fifty examples of the anthem, a through-composed setting of a text which is usually a prose passage from Scripture. The most elaborate of the musical genres favored by New England singing-masters during the latter part of the eighteenth century, the New England anthem (like the Anglican anthem from which it was derived) was intended for choral rather than congregational singing. Anthems by Billings and his contemporaries made use of contrasting chordal and imitative sections and of passages for full choir alternating with passages for one or two parts.

About the text and music

I Am Come into My Garden, I Charge You, O Ye Daughters of Jerusalem, and *I Am the Rose of Sharon* are three anthems all based upon texts from The Song of Solomon: together they form an extraordinary group of Biblical love songs. In these three works are found most of the characteristics of Billings' style—a penchant for melodic writing in each of the parts, sensitivity to the text, and an abundant sprinkling of unorthodox harmonies, including a direct cross relation (in *I Am Come into My Garden,* measure 109), open-fifth cadences, and frequent sets of parallel fifths and octaves. Billings' rhythmic inventiveness appears to best advantage in *I Charge You,* where we find changing meters, Scotch-snap motives, and a syncopated effect on the word "please" at the end of each statement of the rondo-like theme.

The text of *I Am Come into My Garden* consists of selected verses—5:1, 2, and 6; 2:5; and 8:14—which develop in dramatic form three images: a sensual garden, an absent lover, and a gathering of friends come to celebrate. The song begins and ends with a direct address to the absent lover. Within this frame are two addresses to the assembled friends ("Eat, O friends . . ." and "Stay me with flagons . . ."). At the center of the song is a dream-vision recounting an unfulfilled meeting with the lover ("I sleep, but my heart waketh . . .").

In *I Charge You,* Billings arranges verses 8:4 and 5:8–12 in the form of a dialogue between the lover, identified as the "fairest among women," and the daughters of Jerusalem, the women of her community. It opens with two commands demonstrating the strength of the lover's affection, "I charge you, O ye daughters of Jerusalem, that you stir not up nor awake my love till he please" and ". . . If you see my beloved, tell him I am sick of love." The mundane question, twice repeated, "What is thy beloved more than another?" prompts two answers from the lover, the first a simple description of her beloved ("My beloved is white and ruddy, the chief among ten thousand") and the second, which builds upon the first, a poetic and triumphant celebration of her love ("My beloved is white and ruddy, the chief among ten thousand, and altogether lovely; His head is as gold, and his eyes are like doves, and his hair is as black as a raven").

36

THREE ANTHEMS FROM THE SONG OF SOLOMON

For *I Am the Rose of Sharon,* Billings combines verses 2:1–5, 7–8, and 10–11, preserving the dramatic situation of a lover waiting for her beloved. She praises to the audience both her own and her beloved's beauty, and she vividly recounts two occasions which they have shared. Next follow two appeals: the lover asks first to be revived (or "stayed") with wine (which is drunk from "flagons") and then to be comforted with "apples" (the Biblical pomegranates, which were considered a proper food for lovers). She then warns her friends, the "daughters of Jerusalem," that they must not disturb her beloved while he sleeps. In the final section, the lover celebrates the arrival of her beloved, recalling how once he awakened her to greet the arrival of spring after the long rains of winter.

For performance

The sources provide no indications of tempo, dynamics, or ornamentation. For modern performance, the editor has suggested slightly quicker tempi for *I Am Come into My Garden* and *I Charge You* than those recommended by Billings in the introduction to *The Continental Harmony* (Boston, 1794). The addition of some vocal ornamentation would be especially appropriate for the repeat of the final section of *I Am the Rose of Sharon.* These anthems can be performed successfully by either a large chorus or a chamber ensemble. For contrast, the unharmonized phrases can be sung by soloists or by a reduced number of singers.

On the sources

I Am Come into My Garden and *I Charge You* appear to be unique to *The Continental Harmony,* Billings' last published collection. *I Am the Rose of Sharon,* the most popular of these three anthems, was first printed in his second tune-book, *The Singing-Master's Assistant* (Boston, 1778), and by 1810 had appeared in at least sixteen other tune-books. It became one of the most popular and widely reprinted compositions to enter the Southern tune-book tradition. The present edition is based on the version printed by Billings in *The Singing-Master's Assistant.*

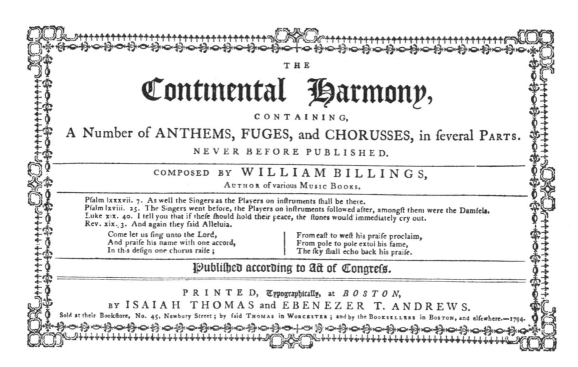

William Billings, *The Continental Harmony* (Boston, 1794), frontispiece and title page (reduced to 70%).

9
I AM COME INTO MY GARDEN

For Mixed Voices (SATB) a cappella

WILLIAM BILLINGS
(1746-1800)

The Song of Solomon 5: 1-2, 6; 2: 5; 8: 14

I have drank__ my wine with my milk.

I have drank my wine__ with my milk.

I have drank__ my wine__ with my milk.

I have drank my wine__ with my milk.

Eat, eat, O friends, drink, drink, O friends.

Eat, eat, O friends, drink, drink, O friends.

Eat, eat, O friends, drink, drink, O friends.

Eat, eat, O friends, drink, drink, O friends.

43

48

49

10

I CHARGE YOU, O YE DAUGHTERS OF JERUSALEM

For Mixed Voices (SATB) a cappella

WILLIAM BILLINGS
(1746-1800)

The Song of Solomon: 8: 4; 5: 8-12

50

51

55

charge you, ___ I charge you that you stir not up nor a-

charge you, I charge you that you stir not up nor a-

charge you, ___ I ___ charge you that you stir not up ___ nor a-

charge you, I charge you that you stir not up nor a-

wake my ___ love ___ till he please.

wake my love till he please.

wake my love till he please. ___

wake my ___ love ___ till he please. What is thy be - lov - ed

more than an - oth - er, O thou fair - est a - mong wom - en?

My_ be - lov - ed is white_ and rud - dy, the chief _____

11
I AM THE ROSE OF SHARON

For Mixed Voices (SATB) a cappella

The Song of Solomon 2:1-5, 7-8, 10-11

WILLIAM BILLINGS
(1746-1800)

As the lil - y a-mong the thorns, so_ is my love ___ a - mong the _ daugh-ters.

As the ap-ple tree, the ap-ple tree a - mong ____ the trees ___ of the wood,

* "Chusing notes:" Basses should divide so that both pitches are sung. When the part is performed by only one singer, the editor recommends that he sing the lower note.

leap-ing up - on the moun - tains, skip-ping up - on the hills.

leap-ing up - on the moun - tains, skip-ping up - on the hills.

leap-ing up - on the moun - tains, skip-ping up - on the hills.

leap-ing up - on the moun - tains, skip-ping up - on the hills.

and said un - to me:

Rise up,

Rise up,

My be - lov - ed spake,

Rise up,

Three Songs

These three brief pieces, written by the Connecticut teacher and tunesmith Stephen Jenks (1772–1856), are in many ways typical of the music composed by New England singing-masters who worked in relative isolation from the European tradition. In these pieces, the singularity of the harmonic progressions (including modal harmonies, harsh dissonances, unusual doublings, and direct cross relations) often appears to be the result of the strong melodic part-writing. Note, for example, the haunting tune of *Sorrow's Tear* and the striking chord progression produced by the melodic tritones in the upper voice of the same composition.

About the texts and music

Sorrow's Tear appears to be a folk-hymn. However, it is not possible to classify it with certainty because the tune has not been identified in an earlier source. *Killingly* and *Weeping Nature* are examples of the plain-tune.

Sorrow's Tear is a setting of a four-stanza poem by Thomas Moore (Irish poet, singer, and composer of popular airs, the best known of which is *The Last Rose of Summer*), to which have been added two anonymous stanzas (5 and 6).[1] Addressing the spirit of a dead child, the singers take the parts of mourners, considering whether to express or to stifle their overwhelming grief (stanzas 1 and 2). The singers confess that although they know life to be as commonly cut short in youth as the morning sun is obscured by daytime clouds, they are nevertheless stunned by the child's death (stanzas 3 and 4). Finally, they contemplate the grave as a suitable refuge from the pangs of "sorrow's tears" which come "when the glitt'ring dreams of youth are past" (stanzas 5 and 6).

In contrast to *Sorrow's Tear*, the anonymous text of *Killingly* is light in tone; it is a celebration of Killingly, Connecticut, a village on the Quinebaug River in the northeastern corner of the state. The scenic beauty of the place forms a "frame" in which a singing soul might find "everlasting bliss."

Weeping Nature employs a text which *The Delights of Harmony* ascribes to "Stennet"—although whether the ascription is to Joseph Stennett (1663–1713) or to Samuel Stennett (1728–1795), both of whom were English hymnodists, is uncertain. However, the latter's popularity among late eighteenth-century American tunesmiths favors the probability that the text is his. *Weeping Nature* deals with the contrast between the natural response to death and the enlightened resignation appropriate to pious men and women who accept the Divine Will. Stanzas 1–4 treat natural phenomena as unenlightened Nature's expressions of sorrow. In stanzas 5–7 the singers reject such open displays of grief, claiming instead that consolation may be achieved for the "true believer" only through steadfast resignation to "God's allrighteous will and mind."

---

[1] Moore's original poem, entitled *On the Death of a Lady*, was published under the pseudonym Thomas Little. The text printed here is based upon the version found in *The Delights of Harmony*.

THREE SONGS

For performance

The sources for these three songs give no indications of tempo, dynamics, or ornamentation. For *Sorrow's Tear* and *Weeping Nature*, the editor has suggested tempi which depart somewhat from the "rule" recommended by most singing-masters that in 3/2 $\downarrow = 60$. It should be noted that the suggested dynamics for these two pieces are applicable only to the first stanza of text. All three songs can be performed successfully by a large chorus, a chamber ensemble, or soloists. In the two plain-tunes, performers may find that the usual octave doublings of tenor and soprano lines are desirable. However, the tune may also be sung by sopranos only and the top part by tenors only, a practice recommended by several singing-masters.

On the sources

Both *Sorrow's Tear* and *Weeping Nature* were first published in Jenks's *The Delights of Harmony*, while *Killingly* first appeared in his *The Harmony of Zion* (Dedham, Mass., 1818). It is upon these sources that the present editions are based.

12

SORROW'S TEAR

For SSB and/or TTB a cappella

Thomas Moore (1779-1852)

STEPHEN JENKS (1772-1856)

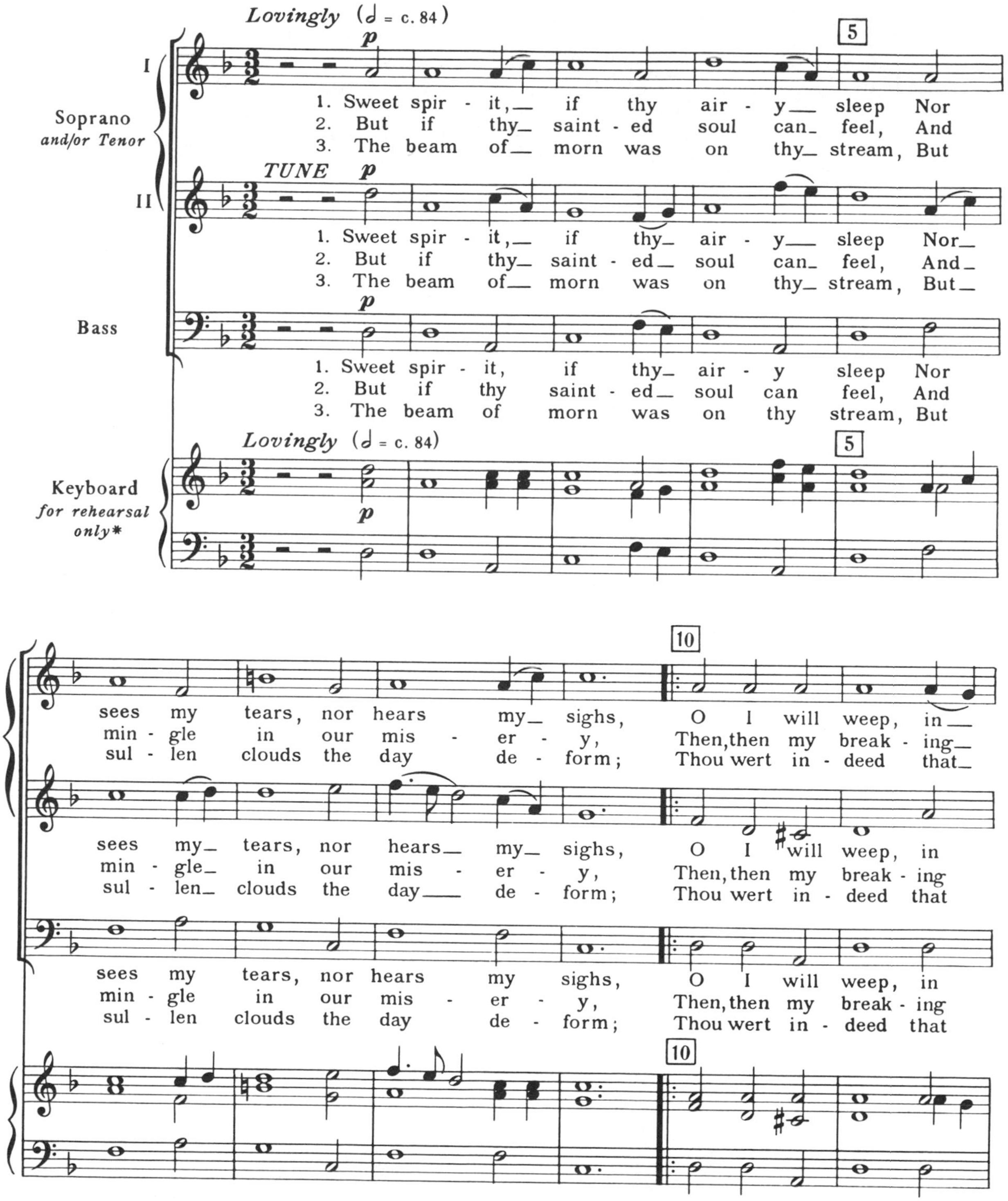

Lovingly (𝅗𝅥 = c. 84)
5
I
Soprano and/or Tenor
II
TUNE
Bass
Keyboard for rehearsal only*
p
1. Sweet spir - it, if thy air - y sleep Nor sees my tears, nor hears my sighs, O I will weep, in
2. But if thy saint - ed soul can feel, And min - gle in our mis - er - y, Then, then my break - ing
3. The beam of morn was on thy stream, But sul - len clouds the day de - form; Thou wert in - deed that
10

* If tenors are used instead of sopranos, the right hand should be played an octave lower.

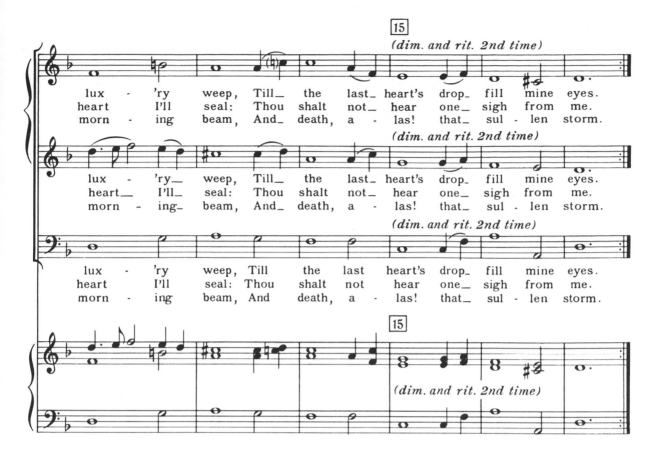

15 *(dim. and rit. 2nd time)*

lux - 'ry weep, Till_ the last_ heart's drop_ fill mine eyes.
heart I'll seal: Thou shalt not_ hear one_ sigh from me.
morn - ing beam, And_ death, a - las! that_ sul - len storm.

(dim. and rit. 2nd time)

lux - 'ry_ weep, Till_ the last_ heart's drop_ fill mine eyes.
heart_ I'll_ seal: Thou shalt not_ hear one_ sigh from me.
morn - ing_ beam, And_ death, a - las! that_ sul - len storm.

(dim. and rit. 2nd time)

lux - 'ry weep, Till the last heart's drop_ fill mine eyes.
heart I'll seal: Thou shalt not hear one_ sigh from me.
morn - ing beam, And death, a - las! that_ sul - len storm.

15

(dim. and rit. 2nd time)

4.   Thou wert not form'd for living here,
For thou wert kindred with the sky;
Yet, yet we held thee all so dear,
We thought thou wert not form'd to die.

5.   How sweetly could I lay my head
Within the cold grave's silent breast,
Where sorrow's tears no more are shed,
No more the ills of life molest.

6.   For, ah, my heart! how very soon
The glitt'ring dreams of youth are past!
And long before it reach its noon,
The sun of life is overcast.

13
KILLINGLY
For Mixed Voices (SATB) a cappella

Anonymous

STEPHEN JENKS
(1772-1856)

79

14
WEEPING NATURE
For Mixed Voices (SATB) a cappella

Stennett

STEPHEN JENKS
(1772-1856)

2. Nature laments the grievous loss,
   Repines and mourns beneath the cross
   Because it cannot be resign'd
   To God our heav'nly Father's mind.

3. Around the coffin Nature stands
   With quiv'ring lips and trembling hands,
   With restless eyes surveys the dead,
   The great destruction death has made.

4. With murm'ring eyes she doth survey
   Her fellow lump of mortal clay,
   Destroy'd by Death's consuming spear,
   The King of Nature's dread and fear.

5. Nature is not subject, we find,
   To the Almighty's sacred mind;
   She cannot say, "Oh, sov'reign Son,
   Thy ways are just, thy will be done."

7. He says, "The heav'nly will be done,
   Thou righteous Lord, eternal Son;
   Thou everlasting God and King,
   Thy will be done in ev'rything."

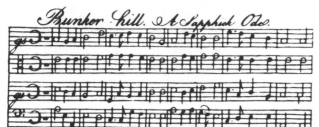
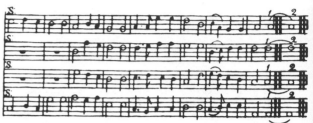

T H E
A M E R I C A N
H E R O
A SAPPHICK ODE.
BY NATH. NILES, A.M.

1.

WHY fhould vain Mortals tremble at the Sight of
Death and Deftruction in the Field of Battle,
Where Blood & Carnage clothe the Ground in Crimfon,
        Sounding with Death-Groans?

2. Death will invade us by the Means appointed,
And we muft all bow to the King of Terrors;
Nor am I anxious, if I am prepared,
        What Shape he comes in.

3. Infinite Goodnefs teaches us Submiffion;
Bids us be quiet under all his Dealings:
Never repining, but forever praifing
        GOD our Creator.

4. Well may we praife him, all his Ways are perfect;
Though a Refplendence infinitely glowing,
Dazzles in Glory on the Sight of Mortals
        Struck blind by Luftre!

5. Good is JEHOVAH in beftowing Sunfhine,
Nor lefs his Goodnefs in the Storm and Thunder:
Mercies and Judgments both proceed from Kindnefs--
        Infinite Kindnefs!

6. O then exult, that GOD forever reigneth
Clouds, which around him hinder our Perception,
Bind us the ftronger .o exalt his Name, and
        Shout louder Praifes!

7. Then to the Wifdom of my Lord and Mafter,
I will commit all that I have or wifh for:
- Sweetly as Babes fleep will I give my life up
        When call'd to yield it.

8. Now, *Mars*, I dare thee, clad in fmoky Pillars,
Burfting from Bomb-Shells, roaring from the Cannon,
Rattling in Grape Shot, like a Storm of Hailftones,
        Torturing Æther!

9. Up the bleak Heavens, let the fpreading Flames rife
Breaking like Ætna through the fmoky Columns,
Low'ring like Egypt o'er the falling City,
        Wantonly burnt down.

10. While all their Hearts quick palpitate for Havock,
Let flip your Blood Hounds, nam'd the Britifh Lyons;
Dauntlefs as Death ftares; nimble as the Whirlwind;
        Dreadful as Demons!

11. Let Oceans waft on all your floating Caftles;
Fraught with Deftruction, horrible to Nature:
Then, with your Sails fill'd by a Storm of Vengeance,
        Bear down to Battle!

12. From the dire Caverns made by ghoftly Miners,
Let the Explofion, dreadful as Vulcanoes,
Heave the broad Town, with all its Wealth and People,
        Quick to Deftruction!

13. Still fhall the Banner of the King of Heaven
Never advance where I'm afraid to follow:
While that precedes me with an open Bofom,
        War, I defy thee.

14. Fame and dear Freedom *lure* me on to Battle,
While a fell Defpot, grimer than a Death's-Head,
Stings me with Serpents, fiercer than Medufa's:
        To the Encounter.

15. Life, for my Country and the Caufe of Freedom,
Is but a Trifle for a Worm to part with;
And if preferved in fo great a Conteft,
        Life is redoubled.

Norwich, (Connecticut) October ---1775.

Andrew Law, *The American Hero,* popularly known as *Bunker Hill* (Norwich, 1775), reduced to 90%.

Six Plain-Tunes

The plain-tune is a four-part musical setting of a metrical text (most often a psalm or hymn) in which all of the stanzas are sung to the same music. The text is usually set syllabically so that the music unfolds in simple chordal style. The six plain-tunes presented here are characteristic examples from the New England singing-school repertory: note especially the strong melodic writing in each of the parts, the open-fifth cadences, and the sets of parallel fifths and octaves. In *Brevity* and *Walpole*, Abraham Wood did not hesitate to use daring harmonies for expressive purposes (see, for example, the augmented-sixth chord in *Brevity*, measure 7, and the biting dissonances of the direct false relations in *Brevity*, measure 11, and *Walpole*, measure 23).

About the texts and music

Of these six plain-tunes, four—*Bunker Hill, Walpole, Funeral Hymn,* and *Newport*—gained considerable popularity in post-colonial America. First published in a broadside in 1775, *Bunker Hill* appeared in at least 18 tune-books between 1781 and 1809. Its text is the only known example of poetic writing by Nathaniel Niles (1741–1828), an inventor, theologian, successful businessman, and liberal politician in state and national government. In the first section (stanzas 1–7) the singers give courage to any who might fear death in battle; in the second section (stanzas 8–13) the singers challenge Mars, the war-god, to a test of courage; in the concluding stanzas (14, 15), they dedicate themselves to freedom earned by noble struggle. For an abbreviated performing version, the editors recommend singing stanzas 1, 8, 10, and 15.

Walter Janes's *Despondency* was published in only two tune-books, his own *Harmonic Minstrelsy* (Dedham, Mass., 1807) and Zedekiah Sanger's *The Meridian Harmony* (Dedham, 1808). The text, from Isaac Watts's *Horae Lyricae* (London, 1706), offers solace to Christians suffering physical decay and death.

Oliver Holden's *Funeral Hymn*, which was included in at least 25 anthologies between 1792 and 1808, is based on a text from Watts's *Hymns and Spiritual Songs* (London, 1707). Similar in spirit to *Despondency, Funeral Hymn* reminds Christians that they are brought closer to God through their suffering.

Daniel Read's *Newport* appeared in more than 35 compilations dating from 1785 to 1810. Like *Funeral Hymn,* its text comes from Watts's *Hymns and Spiritual Songs.* In *Newport* the singers recount a conversion experience: they address the seductions of the World, recalling how "the tempters of the mind" led from easy pleasures "down to the gulf of black despair" (stanzas 1 and 2). The singers then address God, praising the grace which restored them to the "endless" pleasures of true faith (stanzas 3 and 4).

Abraham Wood's *Brevity*, which seems to be unique to Daniel Belknap's *The Evangelical Harmony* (Boston, 1800) is based on an anonymous text which echoes the Service for the Burial of the Dead in *The Book of Common Prayer.* It treats death as the natural end of life.

Walpole, another plain-tune by Abraham Wood, was originally published in the anonymous *Worcester Collection* (Worcester, Mass., 1786); by 1810 it had appeared in no fewer than 40 tune-books. Its text, taken from Isaac Watts's *Hymns and Spiritual Songs,* presents in its first stanza the dramatic situation of a sinner at the moment of true repentance. Directly addressing his own soul (stanzas 2 and 3), the sinner explores the meaning of the Savior's sacrifice, identifying his own lusts and sins with the murderers of Christ. The sinner then turns to address the Savior (stanzas 4 and 5), vowing to renounce the sins and all other "guilty things" by which the crucifixion has been continued down through the generations.

For performance

Except for the two markings in *Funeral Hymn,* the sources give no indications of tempo, dynamics, or ornamentation. For four of these plain-tunes the editor has suggested tempi that depart somewhat from the "rule" given by most singing-masters that in cut time ♩ = 60. It should be noted that the dynamics suggested by the editor for each piece are applicable only to the texts of the first stanzas. These plain-tunes can be performed by a large chorus, a chamber ensemble, or soloists. Some performers may find that the usual octave doublings of the tenor and soprano lines are desirable. Other ensembles may achieve a better sonority by having the tune sung only by sopranos and the top part only by tenors, a practice recommended by several singing-masters. In addition, the Western Wind has found *Bunker Hill* to be effective not only in the SATB version published here but also in a TTBB arrangement in which the top line and tune are sung by tenors and the remaining parts by basses.

On the sources

With the exception of *Walpole,* the present editions of these plain-tunes are based on the earliest known publication of each piece: *Bunker Hill* in an anonymous Norwich (Conn.) broadside of 1775,[1] *Despondency* in Janes's *Harmonic Minstrelsy, Funeral Hymn* in Holden's *American Harmony* (Boston, 1792), *Newport* in Read's *The American Singing-Book* (New Haven, 1785) and *Brevity* in Belknap's *The Evangelical Harmony.* The present edition of *Walpole* is based on the version found in *The Columbian Harmony* (Boston, 1793), the tune-book which, edited by Wood and Joseph Stone, is the only source for this piece in which the composer is known to have had a hand. Stanzas 3, 4, and 5 of *Newport* and *Walpole* do not appear in the original tune-books and have been taken from Watts's original publication. Stanza 6 of each, a Gloria Patri or lesser Doxology, is not part of the original text. It is found in early editions of Watts (both English and American), grouped with other metrical doxologies, and is added here because the music requires an even number of stanzas. (Alternatively, one of the earlier stanzas could be omitted.)

---

[1] Law copyrighted the tune and published it in his *Select Number of Plain Tunes* (n.p., 1781). From surviving evidence, it is not possible to conclude with certainty that *Bunker Hill* is actually by Law; nevertheless, most present-day scholars assign the piece to him.

15
BUNKER HILL

For Mixed Voices (SATB) a cappella

Nathaniel Niles
(1741-1828)

ANDREW LAW(?)
(1748-1821)

2. Death will invade us by the means appointed,
   And we must all bow to the King of Terrors;
   Nor am I anxious, if I am prepared,
   What shape he comes in.

3. Infinite goodness teaches us submission,
   Bids us be quiet under all his dealings:
   Never repining, but forever praising
   God, our Creator.

4. Well may we praise him; all his ways are perfect,
   Though a resplendence, infinitely glowing,
   Dazzles in glory on the sight of mortals
   Struck blind by luster!

5. Good is Jehovah in bestowing sunshine,
   Nor less his goodness in the storm and thunder;
   Mercies and judgments both proceed from kindness-
   Infinite kindness!

6. O then exult that God forever reigneth
   Clouds, which around him hinder our perceptions,
   Bind us the stronger; O exalt his name and
   Shout louder praises!

7. Then, to the wisdom of my Lord and Master,
   I will commit all that I have or wish for:
   Sweetly as babes sleep will I give my life up
   When call'd to yield it.

9. Up the bleak heavens let the spreading flames rise,
   Breaking like Etna through the smoky columns,
   Low'ring like Egypt o'er the falling city,
   Wantonly burnt down.

10. While all their hearts quick palpitate for havoc,
    Let slip your bloodhounds named the British lions,
    Dauntless as death stares, nimble as the whirlwind,
    Dreadful as demons!

11. Let oceans waft on all your floating castles,
    Fraught with destruction, horrible to nature;
    Then, with your sails fill'd by a storm of vengeance,
    Bear down to battle.

12. From the dire caverns made by ghostly miners
    Let the explosion, dreadful as volcanoes,
    Heave the broad town, with all its wealth and people,
    Quick to destruction!

13. Still shall the banner of the King of Heaven
    Never advance where I'm afraid to follow;
    Where that precedes me with an open bosom,
    War, I defy thee.

14. Fame and dear freedom lure me on to battle,
    While a fell despot, grimmer than a death's-head,
    Stings me with serpents fiercer than Medusa's,
    To the encounter.

15. Life, for my country and the cause of freedom,
    Is but a trifle for a worm to part with;
    And if preservèd in so great a contest,
    Life is redoubled.

16
DESPONDENCY

For Mixed Voices (SATB) a cappella

Isaac Watts
(1674-1748)

WALTER JANES
(1779-1827)

* "Chusing notes": Sopranos should divide so that both pitches are sung. When the part is performed by only one singer, either note may be sung.

2. But I forbid my sorrows now;
   Nor dares the flesh complain:
   Diseases bring their profits too;
   The joy o'ercomes the pain.

4. Faith almost changes into sight,
   While from afar she spies
   Her fair inheritance, in light
   Above created skies.

5. Had but the prison walls been strong
   And firm without a flaw,
   In darkness she had dwelt too long
   And less of glory saw.

6. But now the everlasting hills
   Through ev'ry chink appear,
   And something of the joy she feels
   While she's a pris'ner here.

7. The shines of heav'n rush sweetly in
   At all the gaping flaws;
   Visions of endless bliss are seen,
   And native air she draws.

8. O may these walls stand tott'ring still,
   The breaches never close,
   If I must here in darkness dwell
   And all this glory lose!

9. O rather let this flesh decay,
   The ruins wider grow,
   Till, glad to see the enlargèd way,
   I stretch my pinions through.

17
FUNERAL HYMN

For Mixed Voices (SATB) a cappella

Isaac Watts
(1674-1748)

OLIVER HOLDEN
(1765-1844)

3. Why should we tremble to convey
   Their bodies to the tomb?
   There the dear flesh of Jesus lay
   And left a long perfume.

4. The graves of all the saints be blest,
   And soften'd ev'ry bed:
   Where should the dying members rest,
   But with the dying Head?

5. Thence he arose, ascended high,
   And show'd our feet the way:
   Up to the Lord our flesh shall fly
   At the great rising day.

6. Then let the last loud trumpet sound,
   And bid our kindred rise:
   Awake, ye nations under ground;
   Ye saints, ascend the skies.

93

18
NEWPORT

For Mixed Voices (SATB) a cappella

Isaac Watts
(1674-1748)

DANIEL READ
(1757-1836)

95

5.   There from the bosom of my God
Oceans of endless pleasure roll;
There would I fix my last abode
And drown the sorrows of my soul.

6.   To God the Father, God the Son,
And God the Spirit, three in one,
Be honor, praise, and glory giv'n
By all on earth, and all in heav'n.

19
BREVITY

For Mixed Voices (SATB) a cappella

Anonymous

ABRAHAM WOOD
(1752-1804)

20
WALPOLE

For Mixed Voices (SATB) a cappella

Isaac Watts
(1674 - 1748)

ABRAHAM WOOD
(1752 - 1804)

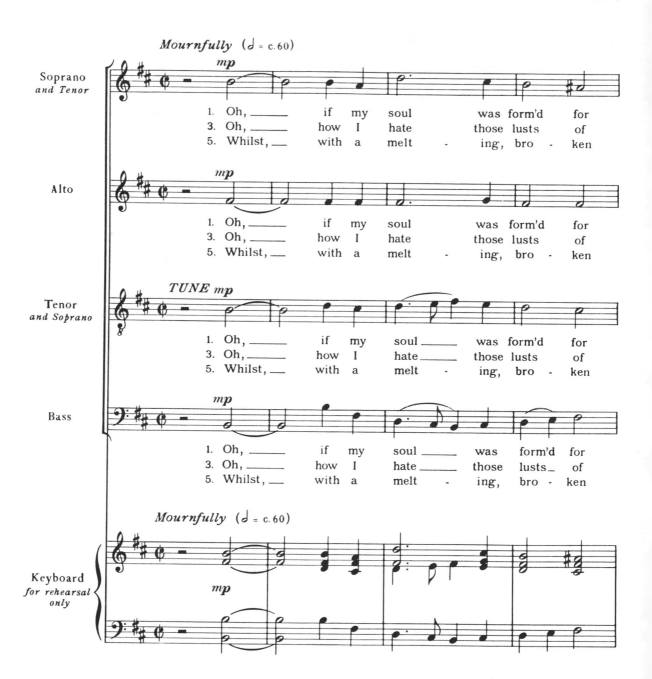

Three Songs of Tribulation

Fidelia, Babylonian Captivity, and *Lamentation* are musical settings of texts dealing with tribulation—affliction, misery, and despair as aspects of religious life. A minor but recurrent theme in American religion, tribulation was especially important in many types of conversion experience common to Puritanism and the revivalist fervor of the Great Awakenings of the 1740s and early 1800s. The three pieces presented here were published in one of the musical monuments of the Second Great Awakening, John Wyeth's *Repository of Sacred Music, Part Second* (Harrisburg, 1813). Some ten per cent of the pieces in *Part Second* may be described as songs of tribulation.

About the texts

The text of *Fidelia* deals with the theme of "religious humiliation." It is taken from verses 4 and 8 of Isaac Watts's metrical paraphrase of Psalm 102 in his *Psalms of David, Imitated in the Language of the New Testament* (London, 1719). Despite the psalmist's feeling of being isolated from the community of the blessed ("far from the tents of joy and hope"), he is yet able to acknowledge the presence of God.

The text of *Babylonian Captivity,* for which no source is known, treats the plight of the faithful, driven in captive bands among idolatrous foes. The popularity of this theme in America may be due to the widespread identification of the Biblical episode with "Indian captivities," pathetic tales of settlers kidnapped by Indians.

The text of *Lamentation* is a metrical paraphrase of Psalm 137 in Tate and Brady's *A New Version of the Psalms of David* (London, 1696). The theme of tribulation is presented in four dramatic outcries: the first four stanzas represent the oppressed captives singing among themselves; stanzas 5 and 6 are directed to the distant city of Jerusalem; stanza 7 invokes God; and the final two stanzas are addressed ferociously to the oppressors, collectively identified as "Proud Babel's daughter."

For performance

Except for the direction "Soft and slow" at the beginning of *Fidelia,* the source gives no indications of tempo, dynamics, or ornamentation. The editor has suggested tempi that depart somewhat from the "rules" recommended by E. K. Dare in his prefatory remarks to *Part Second.* Moreover, in *Fidelia* the editor has substituted common time for the original cut time, and in *Babylonian Captivity* cut time for the original common time (second mood). In these two pieces alternate barring has been provided to clarify the intended rhythmic groupings. It should be noted that in *Lamentation* the suggested dynamics are applicable only to the text of the first two stanzas. These pieces can be performed successfully by a large chorus, a chamber ensemble, or soloists. The editor has scored the upper parts of *Fidelia* (which the source gives in the treble clef) for tenors. However, both tenor parts may be sung

104

by sopranos instead of tenors (as called for in the source), or tenors may be doubled by sopranos. In the two SATB pieces, some performers may find that the usual octave doublings of the tenor and soprano lines are successful. Other ensembles may achieve a better sonority by having the tune sung by sopranos only and the top part by tenors only, a practice recommended by several singing-masters.

On the sources

The present editions of *Fidelia, Babylonian Captivity,* and *Lamentation* are based upon the versions found in the second edition of *Wyeth's Repository, Part Second* (Harrisburg, 1820), which marks the first publication of *Fidelia* and *Babylonian Captivity. Lamentation* had been previously published in Walter Janes's *Massachusetts Harmony* (Boston, 1803). Stanzas 3 to 9 of *Lamentation* (which do not appear in *Part Second*) are taken from the second edition of Tate and Brady (London, 1698). Stanza 10, a Gloria Patri or lesser Doxology, is not part of the original text. It is found in early editions of Tate and Brady grouped with other metrical doxologies, and is added here because the music requires an even number of stanzas. (Alternatively, one of the earlier stanzas could be omitted.)

21
FIDELIA
For TTB and/or SSB a cappella

Isaac Watts
(1674-1748)

LEWER
(fl. c. 1800)

Plaintively (♩ = 84)

Soft and slow

Tenor *and/or Soprano*

Bass

Keyboard *for rehearsal only *

As on some lone - ly build - ing's top The sparrow tells her moan, Far from the tents

* If sopranos are used instead of tenors, the right hand should be played an octave higher.

109

22
BABYLONIAN CAPTIVITY
For Mixed Voices (SATB) a cappella

Anonymous

ELKANAH KELSAY DARE
(1782-1826)

Lyrics (as sung):

A - long the banks where Ba - bel's cur - rent flows,
Our cap - tive bands in deep de - spon - dence stray'd;

110

23
LAMENTATION
For Mixed Voices (SATB) a cappella

Tate and Brady
Psalm 137

Anonymous

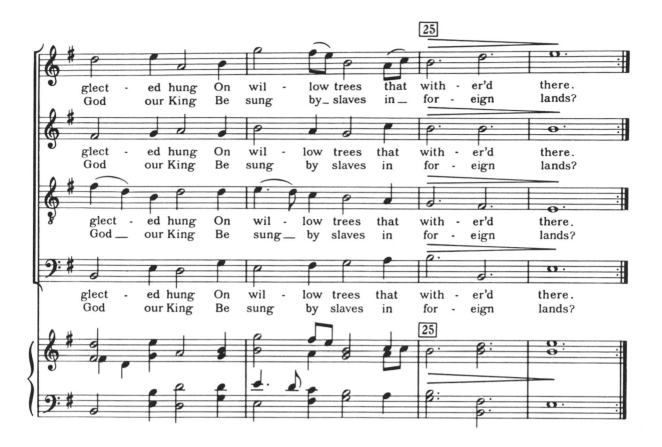

glect - ed hung On wil - low trees that with - er'd there.
God our King Be sung by_ slaves in _ for - eign lands?

glect - ed hung On wil - low trees that with - er'd there.
God our King Be sung by slaves in for - eign lands?

glect - ed hung On wil - low trees that with - er'd there.
God _ our King Be sung_ by slaves in for - eign lands?

glect - ed hung On wil - low trees that with - er'd there.
God our King Be sung by slaves in for - eign lands?

5. O Salem, our once happy seat!
   When I of thee forgetful prove,
   Let then, let then,
   Let then my trembling hand forget
   The speaking strings with art to move!

6. If I to mention thee forbear,
   Eternal silence seize my tongue;
   Or if I sing one cheerful air
   Till thy deliv'rance is my song.

7. Remember, Lord, how Edom's race,
   In thy own city's fatal day,
   Cried out, cried out,
   Cried out, "Her stately walls deface,
   And with the ground quite level lay."

8. Proud Babel's daughter, doom'd to be
   Of grief and woe the wretched prey,
   Bless'd is the man who shall to thee
   The wrongs thou lay'st on us repay.

9. Thrice bless'd who with just rage possess'd
   And deaf to all the parents' moans,
   Shall snatch, shall snatch,
   Shall snatch thy infants from the breast
   And dash their heads against the stones.

10. To Father, Son, and Holy Ghost,
    The God whom earth and heav'n adore,
    Be glory as it was of old,
    Is now, and shall be evermore.

115

Two Settings of Texts on the Theme of Judgment

Samuel Holyoke's *Sandusky* and Justin Morgan's *Judgment Anthem* are musical settings of texts that deal with the Day of Judgment. The Apocalypse was an important theme for composers of the New England singing-school tradition in the late eighteenth century. The popularity of this topic increased at the onset of the Second Great Awakening with its stress on the imagery of hell-fire and brimstone.

About the texts and music

Sandusky appeared in only two early American tune-books, *The Massachusetts Compiler* (Boston, 1795)—a collection published by Holyoke, Oliver Holden, and Hans Gram—and Elisha West's *The Musical Concert* (Northampton, 1807). The music of *Sandusky* reflects Holyoke's knowledge of traditional European harmony: it contains few of the open-fifth cadences, sets of parallel fifths and octaves, and other unorthodox harmonies found in the repertory of the Yankee tunesmiths. In its strophic structure, it resembles a plain-tune, but it is longer and more elaborate than most examples of this genre.

The text of *Sandusky* is composed of lines from hymns by John Cennick (1752) and Charles Wesley (1758). These lines first appear assembled in their present form in Martin Madan's *Collection of Psalms and Hymns* (London, 1760). The version used by Holyoke is based upon the slightly modified version of Madan's text printed by John Rippon in his *A Selection of Hymns from the Best Authors* (first American edition, New York, 1792). The first four stanzas of *Sandusky* vividly describe scenes from the Last Judgment, while stanzas 5 and 6 are addressed directly to God by the congregation of worshippers, which identifies itself as "thine own bride." The worshippers ask that the Savior come quickly and make real the awesome vision they have imagined.

The *Judgment Anthem* was first published in Asahel Benham's *Federal Harmony* (New Haven, 1790). By 1810, it had appeared in at least 23 tune-book editions, and it continued to be printed in collections of the Southern tradition. The *Judgment Anthem* is one of the most remarkable achievements of the eighteenth-century singing-school tradition. Unusually daring harmonic and melodic effects are used to portray vividly the dramatic events associated with the Day of Judgment. The sudden changes of key signature from E minor to E-flat major (measures 44–45, 88–89, and 185–186) and from E-flat major back to E minor (measures 72–73 and 112–113) may appear to result from the composer's inability to indicate the key signatures for parallel major and minor. However, the boldness of the modulations which his notation represents is quite consistent with other features of his style, e.g., wide melodic leaps (tenor, measures 13–14, 82, 175) and striking dissonances (measures 110, 134–135, 170). While such key changes were unusual during this period, they were not unique to the *Judgment Anthem*. (Cf., for example, *New England* by G. Wheeler in *The Musical Medley* [Dedham, Mass., 1808].)

Morgan assembled the text of the *Judgment Anthem* by painstakingly selecting and then re-arranging portions of at least five separate hymns (by Charles Wesley, John Cennick, and anonymous authors) and an ode (by Isaac Watts), all on the theme of the Apocalypse. These texts he found printed in a section of *A Choice Collection of Hymns and Spiritual Songs* (New London, Conn., 1774), compiled by the Mohican Presbyterian clergyman Samson Occom. Like the eighteenth-century American quiltmakers, Morgan imposed a consistent organizing scheme upon the patchwork of rhetorical devices and narrative fragments which he found in his sources. Using the repeated commands "hark," "see," and "hear," as well as narration in the present tense, Morgan created for his singers and their audience a sense of participation in the events described. The anthem begins with the "roar" of Gabriel's trumpet and the appearance of Christ as the Eternal Judge: the souls of mankind are then gathered together by the Archangel, the "Christless souls" are dismissed to everlasting flames, and the saved—the "ransomed sinners"—are summoned to the palace of God, where the anthem concludes with praises for Christ's eternal love.

For performance

The unusually detailed tempo and dynamic markings given for *Sandusky* in *The Massachusetts Compiler* are here printed in roman type. The editor has suggested a tempo somewhat faster than the "rule" indicated by most singing-masters that in common time (first mood) $\quad$ = 60. The editor's source for the *Judgment Anthem* gives no indications of tempo or dynamics. The editor has suggested a tempo somewhat quicker than the $\quad$ = 60 recommended by E. K. Dare in his prefatory remarks to *Part Second*. *Sandusky* and the *Judgment Anthem* can be performed successfully by a large chorus or a chamber ensemble. In addition, *Sandusky* can be sung by soloists. It is a piece which the Western Wind has found to be particularly effective when sung by alto, tenor, and bass. In the present edition, therefore, the upper parts have been notated an octave lower than the original has them, while the part originally given in the bass clef remains the basses'. For contrast, the unharmonized phrases in the *Judgment Anthem* can be sung by soloists or by a reduced number of singers. The editor suggests these special doublings and voicings:

> S doubled by T at the octave: measures 3–7, 62–63, 177–185
> S doubled by B (two octaves below): measures 177–185   (if T doubling is also used)
> T doubled by B (in unison): measures 123–126
> SATB replaced by TATB: measures 186–197, first time only

On the sources

The present edition of *Sandusky* is based upon the version found in *The Massachusetts Compiler*. Stanzas 2 through 6 do not appear in this tune-book, and are taken from the American edition of Rippon's publication. The present edition of the *Judgment Anthem* is based upon the version found in the second edition of *Wyeth's Repository of Sacred Music, Part Second* (Harrisburg, 1820). There is no evidence that Morgan himself supervised any of the publications of his music. Lacking a manuscript or print in which Morgan is known to have had a hand, the editor has selected *Part Second* for his source since the version printed there became a model for collections of the Southern tradition.

24
SANDUSKY

For Mixed Voices (ATB) a cappella

John Cennick
(1718-1755)
Charles Wesley
(1707-1788)

SAMUEL HOLYOKE
(1762-1820)

* "Chusing notes": Tenors should divide so that both pitches are sung. When the part is performed by only one singer, either note may be sung.

* In measures 24-25 of the original source, the bass part is silent. The bass notes printed here appear in the top voice, while the alto and tenor notes printed here appear together in the middle voice.

3. Ev'ry island, sea, and mountain,
   Heav'n and earth shall flee away;
   All who hate him must, confounded,
   Hear the trump proclaim the day:
   Come to judgment!
   Come to judgment! come away!

4. Now redemption, long expected,
   See in solemn pomp appear!
   All his saints, by man rejected,
   Now shall meet him in the air!
   Hallelujah!
   See the day of God appear!

5. Answer thine own bride and spirit;
   Hasten, Lord, the gen'ral doom!
   The new heav'n and earth t'inherit,
   Take thy pining exiles home:
   All creation
   Travails, groans, and bids thee come!

6. Yea! amen! let all adore thee,
   High on thine exalted throne!
   Savior, take the pow'r and glory:
   Claim the kingdoms for thine own!
   O come quickly,
   Hallelujah! come, Lord, come!

25

JUDGMENT ANTHEM

For Mixed Voices (SATB) a cappella

Adapted from Isaac Watts,
Charles Wesley, John Cennick,
and anonymous texts

JUSTIN MORGAN
(1747-1798)

124

* "Chusing notes:" Basses should divide so that both pitches are sung. When the part is performed by only one singer, the editor recommends that he sing the lower note.

roll.

roll.

roll.

roll.

Hear the sound of Christ vic - to - ri-ous; Lo, he breaks through yon - der cloud.

Midst ten thou - sand, thou - sand, thou - sand, thou - sand saints

and an - gels, See the cru - ci - fi - ed shine.

Is that he who died on Cal - v'ry, That was pierc - ed with the

spear? Tell us, ser - aphs, you that won - der'd; See, he ris - es through the air: Hail him.

126

All ye na - tions

All ye na - tions

now de - ter - min'd Ev - 'ry e - vil to __ de - stroy.

now shall sing him Songs of ev - er - last - ing joy.

now shall sing him Songs of ev - er - last - ing joy.

130

131

132

134

135

138

hand a - ris - ing, Fill'd with ven - geance on his foes; _____

Down to hell, there's no re - demp - tion, Ev - 'ry Christ - less soul must go;

Down to hell, there's no re - demp - tion, Ev - 'ry Christ - less soul must go;

* In the early sources, the alto part lacks music and text for "flames."

Hear the Sav - ior's words of mer - cy: "Come, you

180

ran - som'd sin - ners, home, Swift and joy - ful in your

185

jour - ney, To the pal - ace of__ your God."

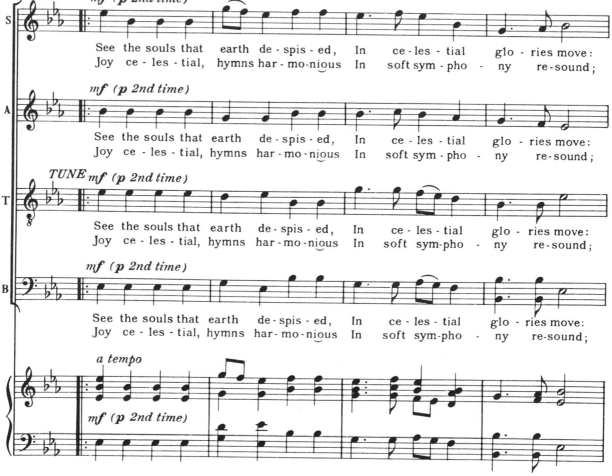

a tempo
mf (p 2nd time)

See the souls that earth de - spis - ed, In ce - les - tial glo - ries move:
Joy ce - les - tial, hymns har - mo - nious In soft sym - pho - ny re - sound;

mf (p 2nd time)

See the souls that earth de - spis - ed, In ce - les - tial glo - ries move:
Joy ce - les - tial, hymns har - mo - nious In soft sym - pho - ny re - sound;

TUNE *mf (p 2nd time)*

See the souls that earth de - spis - ed, In ce - les - tial glo - ries move:
Joy ce - les - tial, hymns har - mo - nious In soft sym - pho - ny re - sound;

mf (p 2nd time)

See the souls that earth de - spis - ed, In ce - les - tial glo - ries move:
Joy ce - les - tial, hymns har - mo - nious In soft sym - pho - ny re - sound;

a tempo

mf (p 2nd time)

Two Songs of Mourning

Columbia and *Lamentation* are funeral elegies which remind both singers and listeners of the experience and meaning of death. Songs such as these were a familiar part of the revivalist camp meetings which played so important a role in the religious life of nineteenth-century America.

About the texts and music

Both *Columbia* and *Lamentation* appear to be unique to Jeremiah Ingalls' remarkable tune-book *The Christian Harmony* (Exeter, N.H., 1805), a collection which contains a large number of folk-hymns—secular folk-tunes to which other voices were added and religious texts were sung. For his secular melodies, Ingalls turned for the most part to familiar British folk-tunes. The tunes of *Columbia* and *Lamentation,* however, have not been traced to specific pre-existent folk-tunes. It therefore seems probable that Ingalls composed the melodies and their harmonies together in imitation of the folk-hymn.

The anonymous text of *Columbia* is taken from Thomas Butts's English tune-book *Harmonia Sacra* (London, [1765?]), and was originally titled *On the Death of Miss R.* The text of *Lamentation* appears to have been published for the first time in *The Christian Harmony.*[1] Although these texts were clearly written for specific occasions (the deaths of "Miss R" and Judith Brock, respectively), the proper celebration of these poignant events could be repeated in song for religious instruction. The texts make effective use of several conventions common to the funeral elegies composed by poets and preachers alike: direct addresses to mourners or bystanders; dramatically conceived speeches directed to or spoken by the deceased; and vividly narrated scenes from the life, death, and projected afterlife of the departed. Each of the songs is powerful because it calls us to witness the importance of one particular dying. For a shorter performing version of *Lamentation,* the editors recommend singing stanzas 1–3, 8, 17, and 18.

For performance

For *Columbia,* the source provides no indications of tempo or dynamics. The editor has indicated a tempo which conforms to the "rule" given by most singing-masters that in cut time ♩= 60. The few original tempo and dynamic markings provided for *Lamentation* in the source have been printed in roman type. The editor has here suggested a tempo somewhat quicker than the singing-masters' "rule" would imply. It should be noted that the suggested dynamics are applicable only to the text of the first stanza in *Columbia* and of stanzas 1–2 in *Lamentation.* These two songs of mourning can be performed successfully by a large chorus, a chamber ensemble, or soloists. The editor has scored the upper parts (which the source gives in the treble clef) for tenors. However, both parts may be sung by sopranos instead of tenors (as called for in the source), or tenors may be doubled by sopranos. The rhythm of *Lamentation* presents many interesting irregularities, including patterns that do not seem to conform to the time signature (see, for example, measures 38 to the end).

---

[1] For information regarding the sources of the texts, the editors are indebted to David Klocko.

26
COLUMBIA
For TTB and/or SSB a cappella

Anonymous

JEREMIAH INGALLS
(1764-1838)

* If sopranos are used instead of tenors, the right hand should be played an octave higher.

146

Fare - well, fare - well, a sad, a long fare - well.

3. In vain the dear departing saint
   Forbids our gushing tears to flow:
   "Forbear, my friends, your fond complaint.
   From earth to heav'n I gladly go
   To glorious company above,
   Bright angels and the God of love."

   Farewell, farewell, a sad, a long farewell.

4. "O praise him and rejoice for me,
   So happy, happy in my God;
   So soon from all my sins set free!
   And hasten to that blest abode;
   With swift desire my steps pursue,
   And take the prize prepar'd for you."

   Farewell, farewell, a sad, a long farewell.

5. "Meet am I for the great reward;
   The great reward I know is mine.
   Come, O my sweet, redeeming Lord;
   Open those loving arms of thine
   And take me up, thy face to see,
   And let me die to live with thee."

   Farewell, farewell, a sad, a long farewell.

6. The prayer is seal'd; the soul is fled,
   And sees her Savior face to face:
   But still she speaks to us, though dead.
   She calls us to that heav'nly place,
   Where all the storms of life are o'er
   And pain and parting is no more.

   Farewell, farewell, a sad, a long farewell.

148

27
LAMENTATION
For TTB and/or SSB a cappella

Anonymous

JEREMIAH INGALLS
(1764-1838)

* If sopranos are used instead of tenors, the right hand should be played an octave higher.

152

the bed, the gar - ments too, All but aug - ment the sore.
while she is call'd a - way; Why this dis - tinc - tion made?

7. Yet you have time; your glass yet runs:
Improve the hours you have.
Perhaps a few more setting suns
Will land you in the grave.

8. All that are tied by nature's bond,
Now can your tears be dry?
Will you not aid my mourning tongue,
Who are but standers-by?

9. She's gone, she's gone, the parents mourn;
She's gone, the children cry,
While my affected bowels yearn
With pangs of sympathy.

10. But yet we need not mourn like those
Who mourn without a hope;
Here is a cordial for our woes,
As a supporting prop.

11. She had a taste for things divine,
But not for carnal mirth;
To those indeed she was inclin'd
Who know the heav'nly birth.

12. She scarce was heard e'er to complain
While she was thus confin'd;
Perhaps to seek would be in vain,
A person so resign'd.

13. Her sickness baffled all the skill
Of doctors, far and near;
Her helpless state that she was ill
Did almost fill two years.

14. Most of the time she thus did lie
And could not turn in bed;
To seek relief in vain they try,
For she receiv'd no aid.

15. Where is the mind remains unshock'd?
Yet view the mournful scene:
Her sore distress with her jaws lock'd;
No food could go between.

16. Thus sev'nteen days she lay confin'd,
And then her life expir'd;
If she in Jesus was resign'd,
Not life could be desir'd.

17. But now we hope she is at rest,
Beyond the reach of pain;
We hope she is with Jesus bless'd,
Upon the blissful plain.

18. Millions of years may roll away;
Our bliss shall still remain.
Our bliss is one eternal day;
It knows not blot nor stain.

"Death, Like an Overflowing Stream": Four Settings of a Text by Isaac Watts

"Death, Like an Overflowing Stream," the text of *Power, Amanda, Mortality,* and *Exit*, consists of stanzas 5–8 of the Ninetieth Psalm from Isaac Watts's *The Psalms of David, Imitated in the Language of the New Testament* (London, 1719). The poetry of Watts enjoyed extraordinary popularity in America during the late eighteenth and early nineteenth centuries. *The Psalms of David* went through more than 100 American printings, the first of which was issued at Philadelphia in 1729. Watts was particularly attractive to composers of the New England singing-school tradition, who drew upon his texts more frequently than those of any other author. Presented here are four of the many settings of one of Watts's most moving texts.

About the text and music

Two of these four compositions gained considerable popularity in post-colonial America: *Amanda* was published in no fewer that 34 tune-book collections between 1790 and 1810, while *Mortality* appeared in at least 25 compilations dating from 1785 to 1808. *Exit* comes down to us in only two collections of the New England tradition, and *Power* appears to be unique to John Wyeth's *Repository of Sacred Music, Part Second* (Harrisburg, 1813). Both *Amanda* and *Exit* were later printed in tune-books of the Southern tradition.

Watts imposed upon his Biblical source (Authorized Version: Psalm 90: 5–7, 9–10, 12) a new structure—that of the religious meditation. The text begins with a powerful imagining of death's force and life's frailty, moving in the second stanza to a quiet consideration of the brevity of life. The third and fourth stanzas contain a colloquy with God: the singers confess their own fear of death and then offer a prayer to God—not for simple longevity but rather for time to acquire the wisdom which is needed to understand and to celebrate both life and death.

For performance

The sources give no indications of tempo, dynamics, or ornamentation. The editor has suggested tempi that depart somewhat from the "rules" recommended by most singing-masters for cut time and common time. It should be noted that the suggested dynamics are applicable only to the first stanza. In *Power*, alternate barring has been provided to clarify the intended rhythmic groupings. These four pieces can be performed successfully by a large chorus, a chamber ensemble, or soloists. For the plain-tunes *Amanda* and *Mortality*, performers may find that the usual doublings of the tenor and soprano lines are desirable. An effective alternative is to assign the tune to the sopranos and the top part to the tenors; this practice was recommended by several singing-masters.

"DEATH, LIKE AN OVERFLOWING STREAM": FOUR SETTINGS

On the sources

The present editions of *Amanda, Mortality,* and *Exit* are based on the earliest
known publication of each piece—*Amanda* in Asahel Benham's *Federal Harmony*
(New Haven, 1790), *Mortality* in Daniel Read's *The American Singing-Book*
(New Haven, 1785), and *Exit* in Daniel Peck's *The Musical Medley* (Dedham,
Mass., 1808). The present edition of *Power* is taken from the version printed
in the second edition of *Wyeth's Repository, Part Second* (Harrisburg, 1820).
Stanzas 2 to 4 (which do not appear in these tune-books) are printed from
Watts's original publication.

28
POWER

For Soprano (and/or Tenor) and Bass a cappella

Isaac Watts
(1674-1748)

WHITE
(fl. c. 1810)

3. But O how oft thy wrath appears
   And cuts off our expected years!
   Thy wrath awakes our humble dread;
   We fear the pow'r that strikes us dead.

4. Teach us, O Lord, how frail is man,
   And kindly lengthen out the span,
   Till a wise care of piety
   Fit us to die and dwell with thee.

29
AMANDA
For Mixed Voices (SATB) a cappella

Isaac Watts
(1674-1748)

JUSTIN MORGAN
(1747-1798)

3. But O how oft thy wrath appears
   And cuts off our expected years!
   Thy wrath awakes our humble dread;
   We fear the pow'r that strikes us dead.

4. Teach us, O Lord, how frail is man,
   And kindly lengthen out the span,
   Till a wise care of piety
   Fit us to die and dwell with thee.

30
MORTALITY
For Mixed Voices (SATB) a cappella

Isaac Watts
(1674-1748)

DANIEL READ
(1757-1836)

morn - ing flow'r _____ Cut down and with - er'd in an hour.
we ar - rive, _____ We rath - er sigh and groan than live.

3. But O how oft thy wrath appears
   And cuts off our expected years!
   Thy wrath awakes our humble dread;
   We fear the pow'r that strikes us dead.

4. Teach us, O Lord, how frail is man,
   And kindly lengthen out the span,
   Till a wise care of piety
   Fit us to die and dwell with thee.

31
EXIT
For Mixed Voices (SATB) a cappella

P. SHERMAN
(fl. c. 1805)

Isaac Watts
(1674-1748)

3. But O how oft thy wrath appears
   And cuts off our expected years!
   Thy wrath awakes our humble dread;
   We fear the pow'r that strikes us dead.

4. Teach us, O Lord, how frail is man,
   And kindly lengthen out the span,
   Till a wise care of piety
   Fit us to die and dwell with thee.

163

Eight Folk-Hymns

The folk-hymn has been defined by Irving Lowens as essentially a secular folk-tune to which a religious text is sung.[1] Lowens suggests that in America an oral tradition of combining a secular folk melody with a sacred text had probably become established by the 1730s. The first printed folk-hymns, however, did not appear until the last decade of the eighteenth century. The eight pieces presented here were first published in John Wyeth's *Repository of Sacred Music, Part Second* (Harrisburg, 1813); four of them—*Washington, Communion, Rockbridge,* and *Fiducia*—were often reprinted in the tune-books of the Southern tradition.

About the texts and music

The publication of the full text of the anonymous *Washington* in *Part Second* suggests that it—like the tune—was new; compilers seldom printed more than the first stanza of a familiar hymn text. In the anonymous poem, a militant believer addresses the Lord, expressing confidence that his own dedication to the "heavenly standard" (described in stanza 1), both in times of religious stress (stanza 2) and in daily experience (stanza 3), will certainly enable him to march in the ranks of the saved at the Last Judgment (stanza 4).

The melody of the anonymous *Spring Hill* is a freely altered version of the middle voice (tune) of *Love Divine,* a three-part piece which was first published in Jeremiah Ingalls' *The Christian Harmony* (Exeter, N.H., 1805).[2] The anonymous text of *Spring Hill* seems also to have been published for the first time in *The Christian Harmony,* where it is printed as an alternative text to *Love Divine. Spring Hill* employs the metaphor of arid land revived by bountiful waters to contrast the secular and the sacred lives. It is addressed to the congregation of the blessed, the "brethren dear, who know the Lord." The singers predict that in heaven "we'll reign, and shout, and sing," promising to renew there the congregational fellowship they embrace on earth.

The melody of the anonymous *Concert* consists of phrases drawn alternately from the two upper voices of a three-part piece bearing the same title and published in Elisha West's *The Musical Concert* (Northampton, 1807).[3] The two-part version printed here is unique to *Part Second.* The text of *Concert* is the popular Methodist hymn "Come, thou fount of ev'ry blessing" by Robert Robinson, originally published in 1759. Robinson's hymn—without its final stanza—was brought out in the following year by Martin Madan in *A Collection of Psalms and Hymns Extracted from Various Authors.* This three-stanza version

---

[1] "Introduction" to the reprint (New York, 1964) of the second edition of *Wyeth's Repository of Sacred Music, Part Second,* p. v.

[2] *Love Divine* appeared with the text "To him who did salvation bring." The melody of both pieces is probably derived from the folk-tune *Nancy Dawson or Miss Dawson's Hornpipe;* see William Chappell, *Old English Popular Music,* new edition by H. Ellis Wooldridge (New York, 1893), II, 186.

[3] The piece published in *The Musical Concert* appeared with the text "Death shall not impede your comfort." It may well be that the melody of both pieces is taken from a common folk-tune source.

had become standard by the end of the eighteenth century, and was used for all subsequent musical settings, including *Concert*. In contrast to the text of *Spring Hill*, "Come, thou fount of ev'ry blessing" is addressed directly to God. Stanza 1 is a call for the divine inspiration which will enable the worshipper to identify himself with God. Stanza 2 attests to the strength of the worshipper's conversion-experience. The "ebenezer" which the singer will raise is a monument set up to commemorate an instance of the Lord's help (see I Samuel 7:12). The final stanza is a prayer for constant faith with which to oppose temptation.

The text of Robinson's *Communion* comes from *Hymns Founded on Various Texts in Holy Scriptures, By the Late Philip Doddridge, D.D.* (London, 1755). Contrasting the poverty of secular satisfaction with the regenerative bounty of religious experience, *Communion* is a call for conversion addressed to the "hungry poor . . . in sin's dark mazes."

The music of the anonymous *Animation* is unique to *Part Second*. The text is the same three-stanza version of "Come, thou fount of ev'ry blessing" that is used for *Concert*. Since, however, the music preceding the "Hallelujah" refrain of *Animation* consumes only half of an original eight-line stanza, the editor has divided the three stanzas of Robinson's text into six strophes. (The addition of a refrain to an established text was a common feature of the Southern tradition.)

The text of Lucius Chapin's *Rockbridge* derives from *Hymns and Spiritual Songs* (London, 1707) by Isaac Watts. *Rockbridge* opens with the dismissal of the mundane distractions which interfere with religious contemplation. Once a mood conducive to a sanctifying experience has been established, the text shifts in the last line of the first stanza to a direct address to the Lord. At the center of this address, which constitutes the remainder of the poem, is an allegorical vision of a feast in which the food served is "heav'nly love" tasting of "truth divine."

The text of Robison's *Fiducia*, like that of *Rockbridge*, is taken from Watts's *Hymns and Spiritual Songs* and deals with a mystic vision—here of God the Father and the assembled heavenly host. The text develops the contrasts between the finite pleasures of earthly religious experience and the "infinite delight" found in God's heaven.

Like *Concert* and *Animation*, the anonymous *Messiah* seems to be unique to *Part Second*, which is also the earliest published source for the anonymous text. The poem follows the pattern of those religious meditative exercises in which the worshipper imagines himself a witness to a sacred event in history and calls upon his soul to re-create the details of the story. The imagined experience—in this case, the Crucifixion of the Messiah—prepares the way for the exalted praise of God which constitutes the eighth and final stanza. For a shorter performing version of *Messiah*, the editors recommend singing stanzas 1, 4, and 8.

For performance

Part Second gives no indications of tempo, dynamics, or ornamentation. The editor has suggested tempi somewhat faster than the $\quad = 60$ in cut time and the $\quad = 60$ in 9/4 that are recommended by E. K. Dare in his prefatory remarks to *Part Second*. For *Washington*, a slower tempo than the $\quad = 120$ recommended by Dare has been indicated. The editor has also substituted cut time for the original 2/4 meter of *Concert*, and has rebarred the music of *Spring Hill* and *Communion* in order to clarify the intended irregular rhythmic groupings. For the same purpose, the editor has provided alternative barring for *Rockbridge*. It should be noted that, except in *Messiah*, the suggested dynamics are applicable only to the text of the first stanza of each hymn. These folk-hymns can be performed successfully by a large chorus, a chamber ensemble, or soloists. *Washington, Concert,* and *Messiah* are folk-hymns which the Western Wind has found to be particularly effective when sung by men's voices. Therefore the editor has scored the upper part of each piece (which the source gives in the treble clef) for tenor. Octave doublings can be used in the remaining folk-hymns. The optional violin obbligato for *Fiducia* has been provided by Stuart Schulman.

On the source

The present editions of all eight folk-hymns are based upon the versions found in the second edition of *Wyeth's Repository, Part Second* (Harrisburg, 1820). Stanzas 3 to 6 of *Communion*, 2 to 6 of *Rockbridge*, and 3 to 7 of *Fiducia* do not appear in *Part Second*. These stanzas are taken from the original Doddridge and Watts publications. Wyeth does not give the full text with the music of either *Animation* or *Concert*; it is, however, supplied with the music of *Shields*, which is the first of the five settings of "Come, thou fount of ev'ry blessing" to be found in *Part Second*. Stanza 8 of *Fiducia*, a Gloria Patri or lesser Doxology, is not part of the original text. It is found in early editions of Watts (both English and American) grouped with other metrical doxologies, and is added here because the music requires an even number of stanzas. (Alternatively, one of the earlier stanzas could be omitted).

John Wyeth, *Repository of Sacred Music, Part Second,* second edition (Harrisburg, 1820), title page and *Concert* (reduced to 70%).

32
WASHINGTON
For Tenor and Bass a cappella

Anonymous   Anonymous

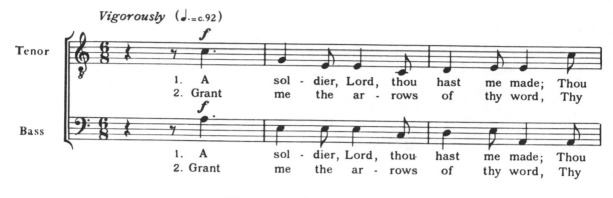

1. A sol - dier, Lord, thou hast me made; Thou
2. Grant me the ar - rows of thy word, Thy

art my cap - tain, king, and head, And un - der thee I
spir - it's pow'r - ful two - edg'd sword, To slay my foes wher -

1. A sol - dier, Lord, thou hast me made; Thou
2. Grant me the ar - rows of thy word, Thy

still would fight The fight of faith all in thy sight.
e'er they be, And own the vic - t'ry won by thee;

still would fight The fight of faith all in thy sight.
e'er they be, And own the vic - t'ry won by thee;

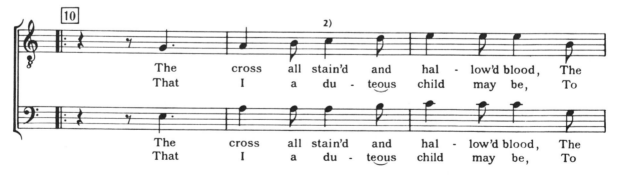

The cross all stain'd and hal - low'd blood, The
That I a du - teous child may be, To

The cross all stain'd and hal - low'd blood, The
That I a du - teous child may be, To

1) Original pitch: e

2) Verse 4: ♪♪♪♩ instead of ♩ ♪ in both parts

168

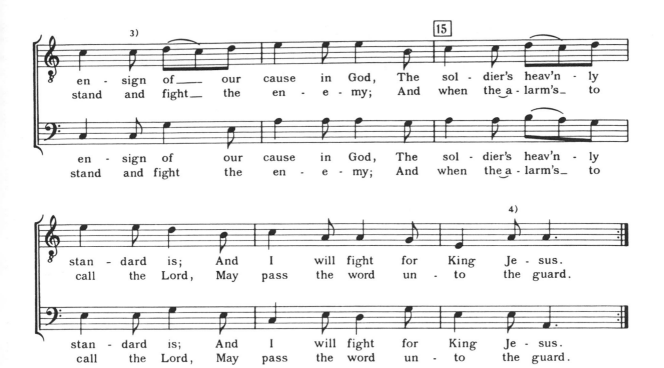

en - sign of __ our cause in God, The sol - dier's heav'n - ly
stand and fight __ the en - e - my; And when the a - larm's_ to

stan - dard is; And I will fight for King Je - sus.
call the Lord, May pass the word un - to the guard.

3. Thou art my guard; keep me I pray,
That I may walk the narrow way,
Nor from my duty e'er depart,
But live to Christ with all my heart.
Help me to keep my guardian dress
And march to the right in holiness;
O make me pure and spotless too,
And fit to stand the grand review.

4. And when our Gen'ral he is come,
With sound of trumpet — final doom;
And when our well-dress'd ranks shall stand
In full review at God's right hand;
It's then the enemy will get the rout,
And wheel'd by him to *left about*!
Then we'll march up the heav'nly street
And ground our arms at Jesus' feet.

3) Verse 3: ♫ instead of ♪ in both parts

4) Original: ♩

33

SPRING HILL

For Soprano (and/or Tenor) and Bass a cappella

Anonymous

Anonymous *

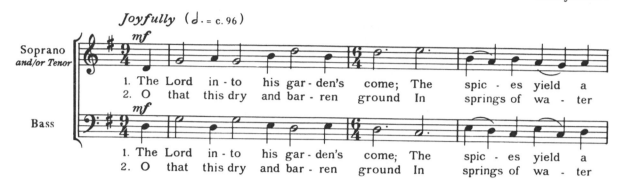

Soprano
and/or Tenor

1. The Lord in-to his gar-den's come; The spic-es yield a
2. O that this dry and bar-ren ground In springs of wa-ter

Bass

1. The Lord in-to his gar-den's come; The spic-es yield a
2. O that this dry and bar-ren ground In springs of wa-ter

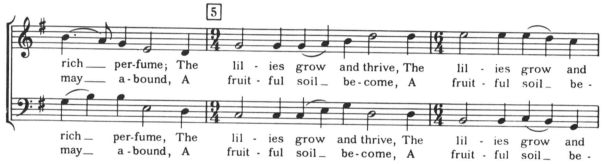

rich __ per-fume; The lil-ies grow and thrive, The lil-ies grow and
may __ a-bound, A fruit-ful soil __ be-come, A fruit-ful soil be-

rich __ per-fume, The lil-ies grow and thrive, The lil-ies grow and
may __ a-bound, A fruit-ful soil __ be-come, A fruit-ful soil be-

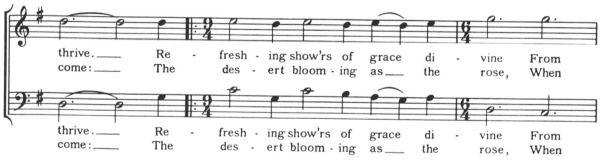

thrive. __ Re- fresh-ing show'rs of grace di - vine From
come: __ The des- ert bloom-ing as __ the rose, When

thrive. __ Re- fresh-ing show'rs of grace di - vine From
come: __ The des- ert bloom-ing as __ the rose, When

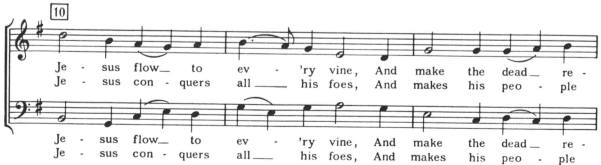

Je - sus flow __ to ev - 'ry vine, And make the dead __ re-
Je - sus con - quers all __ his foes, And makes his peo - ple

Je - sus flow __ to ev - 'ry vine, And make the dead __ re-
Je - sus con - quers all __ his foes, And makes his peo - ple

* Adaptation of a tune published by Jeremiah Ingalls in *The Christian Harmony* (Exeter, N.H., 1805).

170

vive, And make the dead re - vive. Re - vive.
one, And makes his peo - ple one. The one.

3. The glorious time is coming on;
   The gracious work is now begun.
   My soul a witness is:
   I taste and see the pardon free
   For all mankind, as well as me,
   Who come to Christ may live.

4. The worst of sinners here may find
   A Savior merciful and kind,
   Who will them all receive.
   None are too vile who will repent:
   Out of one sinner legions went;
   The Lord did him relieve.

5. Come, brethren dear, who know the Lord,
   And taste the sweetness of his word;
   In Jesus' ways go on.
   Our troubles and our trials here
   Will only make us richer there,
   When we arrive at home.

6. We feel that heav'n is now begun;
   It issues from the sparkling throne,
   From Jesus' throne on high.
   It comes in floods we can't contain;
   We drink, and drink, and drink again,
   And yet we still are dry.

7. But when we come to dwell above,
   And all surround the throne of love,
   We'll drink a full supply.
   Jesus will lead his armies through
   To living fountains where they flow,
   That never will run dry.

8. 'Tis there we'll reign, and shout, and sing,
   And make the upper regions ring,
   When all the saints get home.
   Come on, come on, my brethren dear;
   Soon we shall meet together there,
   For Jesus bids us come.

9. Amen, amen, my soul replies;
   I'm bound to meet him in the skies,
   And claim my mansion there.
   Now here's my heart, and here's my hand,
   To meet you in that heav'nly land,
   Where we shall part no more.

34
CONCERT
For Tenor (and/or Soprano) and Bass a cappella

Robert Robinson
(1735-1790)

Anonymous

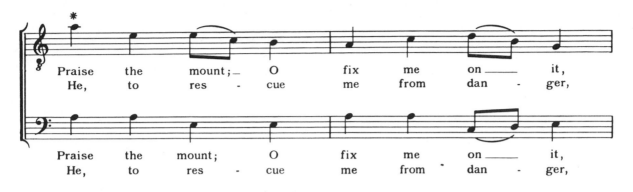

Praise the mount;— O fix me on____ it,
He, to res - cue me from dan - ger,

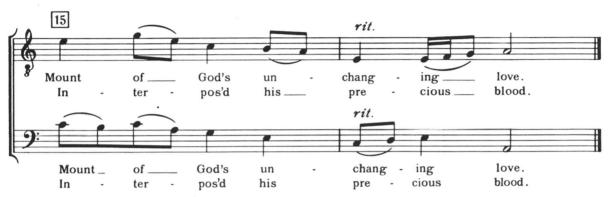

Mount of___ God's un - chang - ing___ love.
In - ter - pos'd his__ pre - cious__ blood.

Mount _ of___ God's un - chang - ing love.
In - ter - pos'd his pre - cious blood.

* The g¹ in the original print is probably an error.

3. O, to grace how great a debtor
Daily I'm constrain'd to be!
Let that grace, Lord, like a fetter,
Bind my wand'ring heart to thee!
Prone to wander, Lord, I feel it;
Prone to leave the God I love.
Here's my heart, Lord, take and seal it;
Seal it in thy courts above.

35
COMMUNION
For Soprano (and/or Tenor) and Bass a cappella

Philip Doddridge
(1702-1751)

ROBISON
(fl. c.1810)

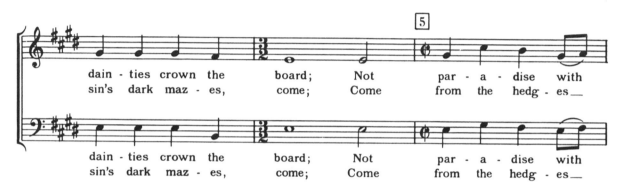

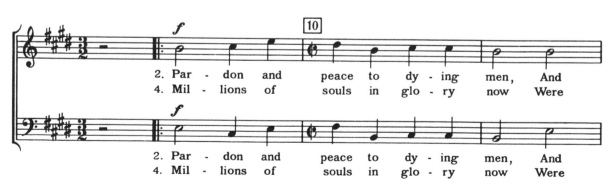

end - less life are giv'n, ———— Through the rich blood that
fed and feast - ed here; ———— And mil - lions more, still

end - less life are giv'n, ———— Through the rich blood that
fed and feast - ed here; ———— And mil - lions more, still

15   *(rit. 2nd time)*   1.   2.

Je - sus_ shed, To_ raise the soul to heav'n.   heav'n.
on the_ way, A - round the board ap - pear.   pear.

(rit. 2nd time)

Je - sus shed, To_ raise the soul to heav'n.   heav'n.
on the way, A - round the board ap - pear.   pear.

5.   Yet is his house and heart so large
        That millions more may come;
        Nor could the wide assembling world
        O'erfill the spacious room.

6.   All things are ready; come away,
        Nor weak excuses frame;
        Crowd to your places at the feast,
        And bless the Founder's name.

36
ANIMATION
For Soprano (and/or Tenor) and Bass a cappella

3. Here I'll raise my ebenezer;
Hither by thy help I'm come;
And I hope, by thy good pleasure,
Safely to arrive at home.

Refrain

4. Jesus sought me when a stranger,
Wand'ring from the fold of God;
He, to rescue me from danger,
Interpos'd his precious blood.

Refrain

5. O, to grace how great a debtor
Daily I'm constrain'd to be!
Let that grace, Lord, like a fetter,
Bind my wand'ring heart to thee!

Refrain

6. Prone to wander, Lord, I feel it;
Prone to leave the God I love.
Here's my heart, Lord, take and seal it;
Seal it in thy courts above.

Refrain

37
ROCKBRIDGE
For SSB and/or TTB a cappella

Isaac Watts
(1674-1748)

LUCIUS CHAPIN
(1760-1842)

Sav - ior see: _____ I _____ wait a _____ vis - it, Lord, from thee.
from a - bove, _____ And _____ feed my _____ soul with heav'n-ly love.

3. The trees of life immortal stand
   In blooming rows at thy right hand,
   And in sweet murmurs by their side,
   Rivers of bliss perpetual glide.

4. Haste then, but with a smiling face,
   And spread the table of thy grace;
   Bring down a taste of truth divine,
   And cheer my heart with sacred wine.

5. Blest Jesus, what delicious fare!
   How sweet thy entertainments are!
   Never did angels taste above
   Redeeming grace and dying love.

6. Hail, great Immanuel, all-divine!
   In thee thy father's glories shine;
   Thou brightest, sweetest, fairest one,
   That eyes have seen, or angels known.

38

FIDUCIA

For Soprano (and/or Tenor) and Bass a cappella
or with violin obbligato

Isaac Watts
(1674-1748)

ROBISON
(fl. c. 1810)

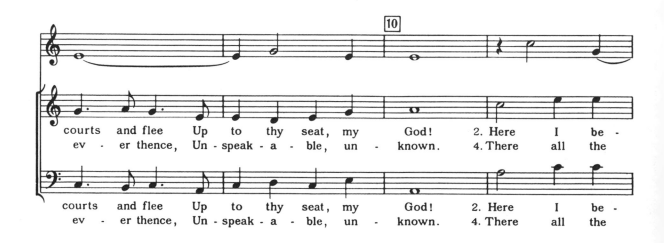

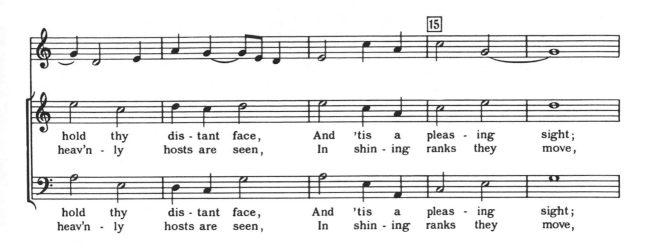

hold thy dis - tant face, And 'tis a pleas - ing sight;
heav'n - ly hosts are seen, In shin - ing ranks they move,

hold thy dis - tant face, And 'tis a pleas - ing sight;
heav'n - ly hosts are seen, In shin - ing ranks they move,

But to a - bide in thine em-brace, Is in - fi - nite de - light.
And drink im - mor - tal vig - or in With won - der and with love.

But to a - bide in thine em-brace, Is in - fi - nite de - light.
And drink im - mor - tal vig - or in With won - der and with love.

5. Then at thy feet, with awful fear,
Th'adoring armies fall;
With joy they shrink to nothing there
Before th'eternal all.

6. There I would vie with all the host,
In duty and in bliss;
With less than nothing I could boast,
And vanity confess.

7. The more thy glories strike mine eyes,
The humbler I shall lie;
Thus while I sink, my joys shall rise
Unmeasurably high.

8. Now let the Father and the Son,
And Spirit be ador'd,
Where there are works to make him known,
Or saints to love the Lord.

39

MESSIAH

For Tenor (and/or Soprano) and Bass a cappella

* "Chusing notes:" Basses should divide so that both pitches are sung. When the part is performed by only one singer, the editor recommends that he sing the lower note.

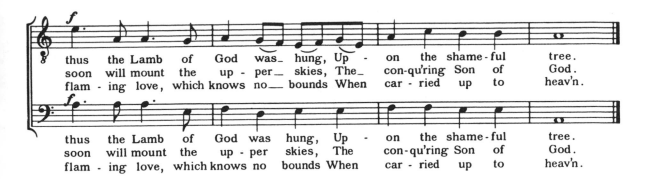

thus the Lamb of God was_ hung, Up - on the shame-ful tree.
soon will mount the up-per_ skies, The_ con-qu'ring Son of God.
flam - ing love, which knows no_ bounds When car - ried up to heav'n.

thus the Lamb of God was hung, Up - on the shame-ful tree.
soon will mount the up-per skies, The con-qu'ring Son of God.
flam - ing love, which knows no bounds When car - ried up to heav'n.

2. T'was thus the glorious suff'rer stood
   With hands and feet nail'd to the wood;
   From ev'ry wound a stream of blood
   Came trickling down amain;
   His bitter groans all nature struck,
   And at his voice the rocks were broke,
   And sleeping saints their graves forsook.
   The spiteful Jews had round him mock'd,
   And laughèd at his pain.

3. Thus hung between the earth and skies,
   Behold him tremble as he dies;
   O sinners! hear his mournful cries,
   Behold his torturing pain.
   The mourning sun withdrew his light,
   Blush'd, and refus'd to own his sight;
   All azure cloth'd in robes of night;
   All nature mourn'd and stood affright,
   When Christ the Lord was slain.

5. Both Jews and Romans in a band,
   With hearts like steel around him stand,
   Saying, if you've come to save the land,
   Now try yourself to free.
   A soldier pierc'd him when he died,
   And healing streams came from his side;
   And thus my Lord was crucified.
   Stern justice now is satisfied,
   Sinners, for you and me.

6. Behold him mount a throne of state,
   He fills the mediatorial seat,
   While millions bowing at his feet,
   In loud hosannas tell
   How he endur'd exquisite pains,
   And led the monster death in chains;
   Ye seraphs raise your highest strains,
   While music fills bright Salem's plains,
   He's conquer'd death and hell.

7. 'Tis done, the dreadful debt is paid;
   The great atonement now is made.
   Sinner, on me your guilt was laid,
   For you I spilt my blood;
   For you my tender soul did move,
   For you I left my courts above,
   That you the length and breadth might prove,
   The depth and height of perfect love,
   In Christ your smiling God.

Three Songs for Men's Voices

Many eighteenth- and early nineteenth-century publications, including the sources for *Triumph*, *Honor to the Hills*, and *Complainer*, do not specify what voices are to sing which lines. Indeed, many pieces may have been intended to be sung by whatever combination was available at the moment. Contemporary evidence indicates that either men or women (or both together) sang the parts written in the treble clef, the men transposing them down an octave. The Western Wind has found that the three pieces presented here are particularly effective when sung by men's voices. In the present edition, the parts originally given in the treble clef are here assigned to the tenors, while those originally given in the bass clef remain the basses'.

About the texts and music

Triumph, which was first published in *Wyeth's Repository of Sacred Music, Part Second* (Harrisburg, 1813), is an example of a three-part plain-tune. *Honor to the Hills* and *Complainer* are two of the many folk-hymns which were published for the first time in Jeremiah Ingalls' *The Christian Harmony* (Exeter, N.H., 1805). *Honor to the Hills* is based on the old English tune *Captain Kidd*, which Ingalls harmonized and used as the setting of a hymn text.[1] The tune of *Complainer*, however, has not been traced to a specific pre-existent folk-tune. It is probable that Ingalls composed the melody together with its harmonies in imitation of a folk-hymn.

For the anonymous *Triumph*, no text source predating the first edition of *Part Second* has been found. The text presents a believer experiencing the sensations of physical death and spiritual rebirth. After hearing the sounds of the "celestials" coming to bear him to heaven, the believer cries out to Nature and the "Bless'd powers" to speed his end, and then, turning to address his grave and the spirit of Death, announces his triumph over them.

The texts of both *Honor to the Hills* and *Complainer* are taken from Joshua Smith's *Divine Hymns, or Spiritual Songs* (eighth edition, Exeter, N.H., 1801), the source for many texts used by Ingalls in *The Christian Harmony*. The text of *Honor to the Hills* bears no attribution in Smith's collection, but in Anna Beeman's *Hymns on Various Subjects* (Norwich, Conn., 1792), it is attributed to Elder Hibard (fl. c. 1790).[2] *Honor to the Hills* declares that "through *all* this world below, God we see *all* around" (italics added). We are given examples of extreme contrasts in nature, all of which testify to God's presence: the lily and the thorn (stanza 1), silent mist and roaring ocean (stanza 2), heavenly bodies and the earth (stanza 3). These illustrations of nature's variety preface two prayers in stanza 4. The first asks for a "station" in life from which the worshipper may continue to rejoice in God's hand in nature. The second introduces the theme of the remaining verses: the special sanctity of hills.

---

[1] For the English folk-tune and its original text, "My name was Robert Kidd," see Bertrand Bronson, *The Ballad as Song* (Berkeley, 1969) pp. 24–33 *passim*.

[2] For information regarding the sources of the texts of *Honor to the Hills* and *Complainer*, the editors are indebted to David Klocko.

Sinai, Olivet, Calvary, and Zion (stanzas 5–8) are singled out as hills which have acquired significance as places where God has touched the earth. Aware of this sanctity, the worshipper prays (stanza 9) for mankind to esteem all hills—even, by implication, the rock-strewn New England hills which Ingalls' fellow Vermonters were often wont to curse.

The text of *Complainer* is ascribed to John Leland (1754–1841) in Smith's *Divine Hymns*. *Complainer* presents the confession of a youthful malcontent who has discovered the humility and satisfaction of true belief. For a shorter performing version, the editors recommend singing stanzas 1 to 5 and 8.

For performance

The sources provide no indications of tempo, dynamics, or ornamentation. The editor has suggested tempi that depart from the "rules" recommended by most singing-masters. It should be noted that in both *Honor to the Hills* and *Complainer* the suggested dynamics are applicable only to the the texts of the first stanzas. In *Triumph,* alternate barring has been provided to clarify the intended rhythmic groupings. These three songs for men's voices can be performed successfully by a large chorus, a chamber ensemble, or soloists.

On the sources

The present edition of *Triumph* is based upon the version found in the second edition of *Part Second* (Harrisburg, 1820). The editions of *Honor to the Hills* and *Complainer* are taken from the readings in *The Christian Harmony.*

40
TRIUMPH
For TTB a cappella

Anonymous

Anonymous

* "Chusing notes": When there are at least two singers on a part, both notes should be sung. For performance by solo voices, either note may be chosen.

41
HONOR TO THE HILLS

For TTB a cappella

Elder Hibard
(fl. c. 1790)

JEREMIAH INGALLS
(1764-1838)

Tenor I/II, Bass, Keyboard (for rehearsal only)

Reverently (♩ = c.69)

1. Through all this world below, God we see all a-round. Search hills and val-leys through: there he's found In grow-ing fields of
4. Then let my sta-tion be here in life where I see The sa-cred Trin-i-ty: all a-gree In all the works he

* Original: **a** (Cf. measure 4.)
** "Chusing notes": First tenors should divide so that both pitches are sung. When the part is performed by only one singer, either pitch may be chosen.

2. See springing waters rise, fountains flow, rivers run;
   The mist beclouds the sky, hides the sun:
   Then down the rain doth pour; the ocean, it doth roar
   And break upon the shore: all to praise, in their lays,
   A God that ne'er declines his designs.

3. The sun, with all his rays, speaks of God as he flies;
   The comet in its blaze, God, it cries;
   The shining of the stars, the moon, when she appears,
   His dreadful name declares: see them fly through the sky
   And join the silent sound from the ground.

5. God did to Moses shew glories more than Peru;
   His fall alone withdrew from the view.
   Mount Sinai was the place, where God did show his grace,
   And Moses sang his praise: see him rise near the skies
   And view old Canaan's ground all around.

6. Elijah's servant views from the hill and declares,
   A little cloud appears, dry your tears.
   Our Lord transfigur'd is, with those blest saints of his,
   As faith the witnesses: see them shine, all-divine,
   While Olive's Mount is blest with the rest.

7. Not India hills of gold, with wonders, we are told,
   Nor seraphs strong and bold can unfold
   The mountain Calvary, where Christ our Lord did die.
   Hark! hear the God-man cry: mountains quake, heavens shake,
   When God, their Author's ghost, leaves the coast.

8. And now from Calvary, we may stand and espy
   Beyond this lower sky, far on high,
   Mount Zion's spicy hill, where saints and angels dwell.
   Hark! hear them sing and tell of their Lord, with accord,
   And join in Moses' song, heart and tongue.

9. Since th'hills are honor'd thus by our Lord in his course,
   Let them not be by us call'd a curse.
   Forbid it, mighty King, but rather let us sing
   While hills and valleys ring, echoes fly through the sky,
   And heaven hears the sound from the ground.

42
COMPLAINER
For TTB a cappella

John Leland
(1754-1841)

JEREMIAH INGALLS
(1764-1838)

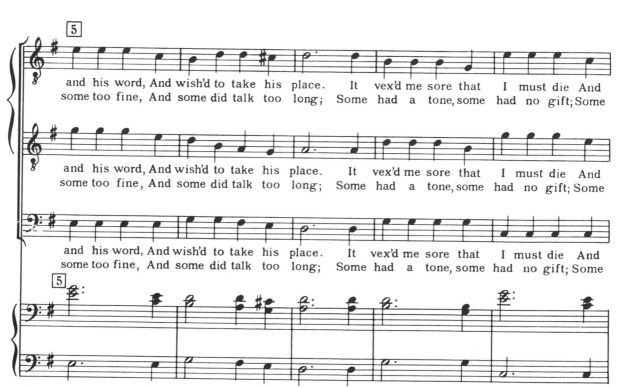

* Original: C (Cf. measure 4)

194

one too low; The oth-ers had no call, The oth-ers had no call.
am-ine me And vex me with their noise, And vex me with their noise.

5. Kindred and neighbors, all were bad,
And no true friends for to be had;
My rulers too were vile:
At length I was brought for to see,
The fault did mostly lie in me
And had done all the while,
And had done all the while.

6. The horrid loads of guilt and shame,
Being conscious, too, I was to blame,
Did wound my frighted soul.
I've sinn'd so much against my God;
I'm crush'd so low beneath his rod;
How can I be made whole,
How can I be made whole?

7. But there is balm in Gilead
And a physician to be had,
A balsam too most free.
Only believe on God's dear Son;
Through him the victory is won:
Christ Jesus died for me,
Christ Jesus died for me.

8. For Christ's free love's a boundless sea:
What! to expire for such as me?
Yes, 'tis a truth divine!
My heart did melt, my soul o'errun
With love, to see what God hath done
For souls as mean as mine,
For souls as mean as mine.

9. Now I can hear a child proclaim
The joyful news, and praise the name
Of Jesus Christ, my King;
I know no sect; Christians are one;
With my complaints I now have done,
And God's free grace I sing,
And God's free grace I sing.

10. Glory to him, who gave his Son
To die for crimes which we had done,
And made salvation mine.
For as we'd sold ourselves for nought,
So without money we are bought.
A blessed truth divine,
A blessed truth divine.

11. Come, saints, rejoice in Christ your King;
His solemn praises sweetly sing,
And tell the world his love.
Sinners invite for to receive
Of God's free grace, and not to grieve
The holy, sacred dove,
The holy, sacred dove.

12. All those who do an int'rest gain
In th' blessed Lamb that once was slain
Will surely happy be.
Their loud hosannas they shall raise,
A monument of God's high praise,
To all eternity,
To all eternity.

Early American Holiday Music

Many compositions found in early American tune-books were written for the celebration of specific religious and patriotic holidays. The present collection offers a sampling of music written for Christmas, New Year's Day, Good Friday, Easter, the Fourth of July, and Thanksgiving.

About the texts and music

The *Redemption Anthem* first appeared in Asahel Benham's *Social Harmony* (New Haven, 1798), where it bears no attribution.[1] After its initial publication, it does not seem to have been printed again until John Wyeth included it in his *Repository of Sacred Music, Part Second* (Harrisburg, 1813). The version published in *Part Second* differs in several ways from the *Social Harmony*'s: common time (second mood) is substituted for 2/4 meter; the opening passage is written for full, four-part choir rather than for bass and tenor only; the repeat is omitted; the conclusion is simplified; and in several passages the harmonies are altered. The *Repository* version appears to have been the basis for later publications of the *Redemption Anthem* in tune-books of the Southern tradition, although their compilers did not hesitate to introduce additional modifications. The anonymous text of the *Redemption Anthem* opens with the re-creation of Christ's birth. Using a technique common in religious meditation, the singers imagine themselves to be present at the sacred event (stanzas 1 and 2). This opening thus builds upon one of the paradoxes of sacred historical events, happenings which occurred once in "real" time, but which believers may re-live time and time again. Stanzas 3 and 4 provide in effectively simple terms a lesson on the significance of Jesus' life. The anthem closes with a prayer for strength to imitate the sacred example of Jesus.

Daniel Read's *Sherburne* was one of the most popular of all early American fuging-tunes and had by 1811 appeared in at least 72 tune-book editions. The text of *Sherburne* is attributed to Nahum Tate, a poet and play adapter whose work, usually done in collaboration, appealed to the popular taste of eighteenth-century England and America. *Sherburne* is a metrical paraphrase of Luke 2: 8–14, reporting the appearance of an angel who announces the Nativity to the shepherds in Bethlehem.

The text of E. K. Dare's *Wilmington* is derived from Charles Wesley's extremely popular hymn "Hark! the herald angels sing." From Wesley's hymn Dare took the first two stanzas verbatim, selecting from the remaining eight quatrains only four couplets, which he re-arranged to form his second and third stanzas. The first stanza is a dramatic call to the world to hear Heaven's celebration of the Nativity. The second stanza, marked "Spirituoso" by Dare, is a command: ". . . all ye nations, rise; join the triumph of the skies." The third stanza ("Moderato" and "Piano") quietly interprets the meaning of the event. Although Wesley's version of the hymn continues with the command to the world "Hail

---

[1] Concerning the probable attribution of this anthem, see the biographical notes on Asahel Benham, p. 259.

the heav'n-born Prince of Peace!" Dare's fourth stanza is directed to the infant Jesus, to whom the singers turn, saying "Hail! *thou* heav'n-born Prince of Peace" (italics the editor's). Dare ends the anthem with a delightful three-fold *laudate* ("Praise ye the Lord"), which he indicates should be sung at first "Slow, soft," then "Crescendo," and finally "Loud."

The text of Oliver Holden's *Christmas,* taken from Isaac Watts's *Hymns and Spiritual Songs* (London, 1707), begins with two commands calling the audience to witness the events of Christ's Nativity. Stanzas 2 and 3 set forth the Infant's regal powers; stanzas 4, 5, and 6 recount the appearance of the angel to the shepherds, and stanza 7 calls upon the congregation to join the saints in singing the Chorus, a prayer for the glory, peace, goodwill, and joy appropriate to Christmas. The composer indicates that *Christmas* may be performed in a shortened version by omitting the Chorus after each stanza. For a modern performing version, the editors recommend singing stanzas 1, 4, 6, and 7, with the Chorus after each.

William Selby's *Ode for the New Year* is among the many patriotic musical works inspired by the birth of the American republic. Paradoxically, however, it departs from the most important American musical style of the late eighteenth century, the New England singing-school tradition: the text is political rather than religious, the melodic writing is more soloistic than choral, and the harmony reflects the orthodox practices of contemporary European composers rather than the rugged part-writing of the Yankee tunesmiths. It is not surprising, therefore, that an ode such as this one appeared not in tune-books but in publications such as broadsides and periodicals. *Ode for the New Year* was first published at Boston in Isaiah Thomas' *The Massachusetts Magazine* in January 1790 and was reprinted in *The American Musical Miscellany* (Northampton, 1798), a collection of more than one hundred secular songs engraved in the standard upright book format rather than in the oblong shape characteristic of the American tune-book. In this anonymous patriotic ode, George Washington receives rhetorical compliments of the sort which in the courtly tradition are normally bestowed upon royalty and which in religious verse are usually reserved for God. The text begins with a series of vigorous commands (stanzas 1 and 2). The sleeping sun, addressed as "Apollo" and "Sol," is ordered to rise and begin the first day of the new year, while "slumb'ring nations" are urged to wake up to greet "today's celestial Prince," a figure identified as George Washington, who is hailed by the populations of America, Europe, Africa, and Asia (stanzas 3 to 6). Continuing fame for both Columbia and "the godlike Washington" are predicted (stanza 7), and the "rolling years" are asked to hasten the arrival of an earthly "bliss" when "ev'ry nation [shall] boast a Washington."

The text of Daniel Read's *Hamshire,* stanzas 1–3 of a six-stanza poem from Isaac Watts's *Horae Lyricae* (London, 1706), re-creates the experience of the crucifixion and resurrection. Briefly the singers re-live the events of Good Friday, stimulating their own emotions of sympathy and grief; they then address their congregation, calling upon the "saints"—the beneficiaries of Christ's sacrifice—to express by weeping the sorrow felt for the Savior's suffering; finally, the singers report Christ's resurrection, thereby evoking the joy of Easter Sunday.

Horatio Garnet's *An Ode for the Fourth of July* is a patriotic piece written shortly after the conclusion of the Revolutionary War. The music, like Selby's setting of *Ode for the New Year,* shows the influence of contemporary European composers. *An Ode for the Fourth of July* first appeared in *The Massachusetts*

Magazine in July 1789 and, like *Ode for the New Year,* was printed again in *The American Musical Miscellany.* The text is by Daniel George (1758–1804), known only as a Massachusetts man and a compiler of almanacs: it reinterprets the emergence of the new American state, presenting its history as a ceremonial progress beginning with the signing of the Declaration of Independence ("Tis done!" stanza 1), continuing through the victories of the Revolutionary War (stanzas 2–5), and culminating in George Washington's election to the presidency. The last stanza foresees the establishment of a flourishing economic community in America, protected by Washington. This vision recalls the utopian theocracies envisioned by the original New England settlers.

The text of William Billings' *An Anthem for Thanksgiving* is a freely rendered version of Psalm 148, verses 1–5 and 7–13, to which have been added both a short passage from Wentworth Dillon, 4th Earl of Roscommon's paraphrase of Psalm 148 and several lines presumably composed by Billings himself.[2] The singers address a remarkably diverse catalogue of celestial bodies, "natural" phenomena, and creatures ranging from "creeping insects" to "dragons" (the description of these last is Roscommon's contribution): all are urged to praise their Creator. In the witty passage by Billings (beginning "Join, creation, . . ."), the singers explain that the entire universe fulfills its purpose when it praises God. The anthem ends with hallelujahs.

For performance

The original tempo and dynamic markings given for *Wilmington, Christmas, Hamshire,* and *An Ode for the Fourth of July* are here printed in roman type. The sources for the remaining pieces provide no indications of tempo or dynamics. For the *Redemption Anthem* and *Wilmington,* the editor has supplied the tempi recommended by E. K. Dare in his prefatory remarks to *Wyeth's Repository, Part Second.* For *Sherburne, Christmas,* and the *Thanksgiving Anthem,* the editor has suggested tempi that depart somewhat from the "rules" given by most singing-masters. It should be noted that in *Christmas* and in the two patriotic odes the suggested dynamics are applicable only to the text of the stanzas that are underlaid. Trills given in the original sources for the two odes and for *Hamshire* have been reproduced here, while appoggiaturas and other ornamentation have been written out.

Although no instruments are mentioned in either *The Massachusetts Magazine* or *The American Musical Miscellany,* keyboard doublings of the vocal lines of the two odes by harpsichord or organ may be appropriate. It should be noted in support of this view that these pieces clearly lie outside the realm of the a cappella New England singing-school tradition, and that Selby himself was an accomplished keyboard player and composer of instrumental music. *Hamshire* is the only piece in the present collection which originally included written-out passages for instruments. This anthem first appeared in Daniel Read's tune-book *The Columbian Harmonist No. 3* (New Haven, 1795), in which source there appear between the stanzas two-part instrumental "Symphonies" which are written on the top and bottom lines of the voice parts. Although Read does not specify the instruments by which the symphonies are to be performed, the writing seems especially suited for strings; the editor has

---

[2] In *The Continental Harmony,* Billings carefully identifies the sources of his texts except when he himself is the author; the lines in *An Anthem for Thanksgiving* which Billings does not credit to any other source are therefore probably his.

accordingly suggested that they be taken by violin and violoncello. Read does not indicate whether or not the instruments are also to play the vocal lines of the stanzas, but the editor has suggested that the vocal lines be doubled, since by the 1790s instrumental doubling in anthems was a rather common practice in New England churches. The editor also suggests that the alto and tenor be doubled throughout; the ranges of the four vocal lines are well suited to the string quartet, with violin II playing the tenor line an octave above the tenors. Various other instruments might be employed effectively. Alternatively, the organ could double the chorus parts and play the symphonies (without, however, filling in the chords). The editor has not regarded the lowest line as the bass of a continuo, since Read himself does not seem to have employed the basso continuo.

Sherburne, Wilmington, Christmas, Hamshire, and *An Anthem for Thanksgiving* can be performed successfully by either a large chorus or a chamber ensemble. *Sherburne* can also be sung by soloists. In *An Anthem for Thanksgiving,* for contrast the unharmonized phrases which appear in alto, tenor, and bass can be sung by soloists or by a reduced number of singers. The *Redemption Anthem,* which in the late eighteenth- and early nineteenth-century sources was scored for a single choir, has here been arranged for double chorus. Alternatively, sections designated for Chorus I may be performed by a quartet of soloists. The two patriotic odes are pieces which the Western Wind has found to be particularly effective when sung by men's voices. In the present edition, therefore, the upper parts have been notated an octave lower than the original has them, while the part originally given in the bass clef remains the basses'. In the three-part sections, the tune should always be prominent.

On the sources

The present editions of the *Redemption Anthem* and *Wilmington* are based upon the readings found in the second edition of *Wyeth's Repository, Part Second* (Harrisburg, 1820). The version of the *Redemption Anthem* in this source contains some obvious notational errors of rhythm and pitch; in these instances, the editor has followed the *Social Harmony* readings. The text follows *Part Second* in all particulars, even in those readings for which it differs from the *Social Harmony.* The editions of the remaining pieces are taken from their first printings: *Sherburne* in Daniel Read's *The American Singing-Book* (New Haven, 1785), *Christmas* in Oliver Holden's *American Harmony* (Boston, 1792), the two patriotic odes in *The Massachusetts Magazine, Hamshire* in *The Columbian Harmonist No. 3,* and *An Anthem for Thanksgiving* in William Billings' *The Continental Harmony* (Boston, 1794). Stanzas 3 to 8 of *Christmas* (which do not appear in the *American Harmony*) are printed from Watts's original publication.

43

REDEMPTION ANTHEM

For Two Choruses of Mixed Voices
(SATB & SATB) a cappella

Anonymous

ASAHEL BENHAM (?)
(1757-1805)

200

* The editor has changed all appearances of the original rhythm ♩. ♫ to read ♩. ♫ ♩.

hills re - ply; Eve - ning re - peats to won - d'ring morn, A

hills re - ply; Eve - ning re - peats to won - d'ring morn, A

Eve - ning re - peats to won - d'ring morn, A

Eve - ning re - peats to won - d'ring morn, A

Chorus I

God, a God on earth is born. Our frail - ties

God, a God on earth is born. Our frail - ties

God, a God on earth is born. Our frail - ties —

God, a God on earth is born. Our frail - ties

long he— deign'd to— share, The heir of heav'n, of
long he deign'd to— share, The— heir of heav'n, of
long he— deign'd to— share, The heir of— heav'n, of
long he— deign'd— to— share, The heir of heav'n, of

pain— the— heir; By mir-a-cles his pow'r he tried;
pain— the heir; By mir-a-cles his pow'r he tried;
pain— the— heir; By mir-a-cles his pow'r he— tried;
pain— the heir; By mir-a-cles his pow'r he tried;

203

O may we strive like him to live: Our
O may we strive like him to live: Our
O may we strive like him to live: Our
O may we strive like him to live: Our

friends es - teem, our foes for - give,
friends es - teem, our foes for - give,
friends es - teem, our foes for - give, Our
friends es - teem, our foes for - give, Our

207

44
SHERBURNE
For Mixed Voices (SATB) a cappella

Nahum Tate
(1652-1715)

DANIEL READ
(1757-1836)
Edited by Lawrence Bennett

208

209

3. "To you, in David's town, this day
   Is born of David's line
   The Savior, who is Christ, the Lord;
   And this shall be the sign:"

4. "The heav'nly babe you there shall find
   To human view display'd,
   All meanly wrapp'd in swathing bands
   And in a manger laid."

5. Thus spake the seraph; and forthwith
   Appear'd a shining throng
   Of angels praising God, and thus
   Address'd their joyful song:

6. "All glory be to God on high,
   And to the earth be peace;
   Good will henceforth from heav'n to men
   Begin and never cease!"

45
WILMINGTON

A Christmas Anthem on the text "Hark! the Herald Angels Sing"
For Mixed Voices (STTB) a cappella

Adapted from
CHARLES WESLEY
(1707-1788)

ELKANAH KELSAY DARE
(1782-1826)

* "Chusing notes": When there are at least two singers on a part, both notes should be sung. For performance by solo voices, the lower note should usually be chosen, unless another pitch is needed to fill out the triad.

* Original: **a**

Christ is born in Beth-le-hem. hem.

Christ is born, Christ is born in Beth-le-hem. hem.

Christ is born in Beth-le-hem. hem.

Christ is born, Christ is born in Beth-le-hem. hem.

3. Christ, by high-est heav'n a - dor'd; Christ, the ev - er - last - ing Lord,

Low-ly lays his glo - ries by, Born for men, for men to die.

Low-ly lays his glo - ries by, Born for men, for men to die.

46
CHRISTMAS
For Mixed Voices (SATB) a cappella

Isaac Watts
(1674-1748)

OLIVER HOLDEN
(1765-1844)

1. Be - hold,— the grace— ap - pears; The prom - ise is - ful - fill'd. Be - hold, the won - d'rous vir - gin bears, And Je - sus
2. The Lord,— the high - est God, Calls him— his on - ly son; He bids— him rule— the lands— a - broad, And gives— him

219

3. O'er Jacob shall he reign
   With a peculiar sway;
   The nations shall his grace obtain,
   His kingdom ne'er decay.

   Chorus

4. To bring the glorious news,
   A heav'nly form appears;
   He tells the shepherds of their joys
   And banishes their fears.

   Chorus

5. "Go, humble swains;" said he,
   "To David's city fly;
   The promised infant, born today,
   Doth in a manger lie."

   Chorus

6. "With looks and hearts serene,
   Go visit Christ, your King."
   And straight a flaming troop was seen;
   The shepherds heard them sing.

   Chorus

7. In worship so divine,
   Let saints employ their tongues;
   With the celestial hosts we join
   And loud repeat their songs.

   Chorus

47

ODE FOR THE NEW YEAR

For TTB a cappella

Anonymous

WILLIAM SELBY
(1738-1798)

1. Hark! notes melodious fill the skies: From
3. Columbia heard the high behest; Her

The tis' lap, Apollo, rise; Thy swift-wheel'd chariot
free born millions smote the breast! And silent slept the

speed, Thy swift-wheel'd chariot speed amain! O'er
heav'n-, And silent slept the heav'n-strung lyre, Till

fleet-ing courses, fleet-ing courses loose the rein! The
Free-dom breath'd, Till Free-dom breath'd impassion'd fire; Till

* Original: a

222

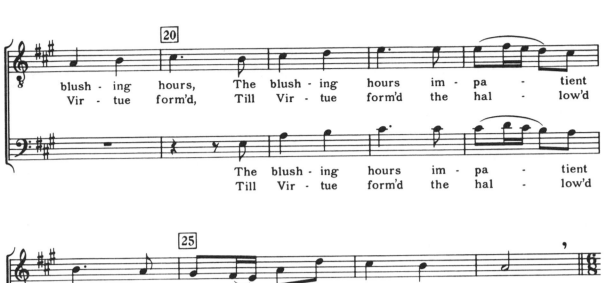

blush - ing hours, The blush - ing hours im - pa - tient
Vir - tue form'd, Till Vir - tue form'd the hal - low'd

The blush - ing hours im - pa - tient
Till Vir - tue form'd the hal - low'd

stand! The vir - gin_ day waits thy com - mand!
sound, And Fame en - rap - tur'd roll'd it round.

stand! The vir - gin day waits thy com - mand!
sound, And Fame en - rap - tur'd roll'd it round.

Chorus
(♩. = c.80)

A - wake, O Sol, and lead_ from e - ther's sphere, In
All hail to Free - dom's, Vir - tue's, Glo - ry's Sun! Ye

TUNE

A - wake, O Sol, and lead_ from e - ther's sphere, In
All hail to Free - dom's, Vir - tue's, Glo - ry's Sun! Ye

A - wake, O Sol, and lead from e - ther's sphere, In
All hail to Free - dom's, Vir - tue's, Glo - ry's Sun! Ye

(♩. = c.80)

Keyboard
*for rehearsal
only*

2. And as the golden car of light
   Refulgent beams on mortal sight,
   As fiery steeds (which oft times lave
   Their wingèd feet in ocean's wave)
   Ascend above the mantling deep
   And rapid gain th'empyrean sleep,
   Let slumb'ring nations rise and loud prolong
   Today's celestial Prince, the choral song.

4. European kingdoms caught the strain:
   From mount to vale, from hill to plain,
   Triumphant shouts with one acclaim
   Re-echoing swell'd the trump of Fame.
   "All hail!" the Gallic peasant cries;
   The cloister'd monk, the nun replies:
   "Illustrious George! Great Patriot Sage! Twas thine!
   To pour on France the flood of light divine!"

5. What notes are these? How grand, sublime!
   Tis freedom's song in Afric's clime!
   The wretch, the slave whom fetters bound,
   Exulting hears the joyful sound;
   Ecstatic transports fire his soul,
   And grateful paeans hourly roll.
   For thee alone he hails the rising dawn;
   The friend of man in Washington was born.

6. Lo, Asia joins the note of praise;
   Her myriads dream of halcyon days,
   When holy truth, with eagle ken,
   Shall scan the rights of fellow men;
   When impious tyrants, hurl'd from pow'r,
   No more shall spoil industry's flow'r;
   But perfect Freedom gild her evening Sun,
   And glow with cloudless, beam-like Washington.

7. Hail, favor'd land, the pride of earth!
   All nations hail Columbia's birth;
   From Europe's realms to Asia's shore,
   Or where the Niger's billows roar,
   On eagle plume thy deeds shall fly.
   And long as Sol adorns the sky,
   Ten thousand, thousand clarion tongues proclaim
   The godlike Washington's immortal name.

8. Oh, rapid post ye rolling years,
   Revolving swift through circling spheres,
   And haste along the promis'd time
   When liberty, from clime to clime,
   With sacred peace and union join'd,
   And virtue blessing human kind,
   Shall equal bliss diffuse beneath the sun,
   And ev'ry nation boast a Washington.

48
HAMSHIRE: For Good Friday
For Mixed Voices (SATB) with Violin and Violoncello

Isaac Watts
(1674-1748)

DANIEL READ
(1757-1836)

228

* Original pitch: d".

233

234

49

AN ODE FOR THE FOURTH OF JULY

For TTB a cappella

Daniel George
(1758-1804)

HORATIO GARNET
(fl. c.1790)

* "Chusing notes": When there are at least two singers on the bass line, both parts in measures 30-31 should be sung. For performance by solo voices, the editor recommends that the notes with down-stems be sung.

** Original: e

3. Let Saratoga's crimson plains declare
    The deeds of Gates, that "thunderbolt of war:"
        His trophies grac'd the field;
        He made whole armies yield —
            A vet'ran band:
    In vain did Burgoyne strive his valor to withstand.
            Chorus:

4. Now Yorktown's heights attract our wond'ring eyes,
    Where loud artill'ry rends the lofty skies:
        There Washington commands,
        With Gallia's chosen bands,
            A warlike train.
    Like Homer's conqu'ring gods, they thunder o'er the plain.
            Chorus:

5. Pale terror marches on with solemn stride;
    Cornwallis trembles, Britain's boasted pride.
        He and his arm-ed hosts
        Surrender all their posts
            To Washington,
    The friend of Liberty, Columbia's fav'rite son.
            Chorus:

6. Now from Mount Vernon's peaceful shades again,
    The Hero comes with thousands in his train:
        Tis Washington the Great
        Must fill the chair of state,
            Columbia cries:
    Each tongue the glorious name re-echoes to the skies.
            Chorus:

7. Now shall the useful arts of peace prevail,
    And commerce flourish, favor'd by each gale.
        Discord, forever cease;
        Let Liberty and Peace
            And Justice reign,
    For Washington protects the scientific train.
            Chorus:

50
AN ANTHEM FOR THANKSGIVING

For Mixed Voices (SATB) a cappella

Adapted from
Psalm 148

WILLIAM BILLINGS
(1746-1800)

240

246

249

251

Pilgrim's Farewell

The figure of the pilgrim, a traveler who has renounced the familiarity and comforts of his secular life in order to journey to a sacred place, held special significance for Americans of the eighteenth and early nineteenth centuries. For settlers in the New World, voyages from Europe to America and treks from the coastal cities to the inland wilderness could easily be seen as forms of pilgrimage in which attachments to worldly societies were thrown off for the purpose of arriving purified in the New Canaan, the holy land prepared for them by God. Read in these terms, *Pilgrim's Farewell* was invested with both religious and secular meaning.

Conflicting attributions make it impossible to identify the composer of *Pilgrim's Farewell*. The composition first appeared in Jacob French's *The Psalmodist's Companion* (Worcester, 1793), where it is anonymous. When French printed the piece again, in his *Harmony of Harmony* (Northampton, 1802), he ascribed it to "Field." However, in Joel Read's *The New England Selection* (Boston, 1808), it is attributed to French. None of the other early sources provides information about the authorship.

About the text and music

The text of *Pilgrim's Farewell* derives from Samuel Crossman's poem "A Pilgrim's Farewell to the World," printed in his *Young Man's Meditation, or Some Few Sacred Poems* . . . (London, 1664). The text is conceived as a valediction spoken by the pilgrim to his community, addressed as "my friends," "my loving friends," "dear brethren in the Lord," and "ye blooming sons of God." The spirit of fellowship reflected here was an important part of the religious camp meetings in the newly settled areas of the United States, where songs such as this were often sung. In the first two stanzas the pilgrim describes his march to "Canaan's shore," the boundary of heaven which is death. In the third stanza he gives consolation to those whom he is leaving behind, and in the final stanza he encourages his friends, for whom "sore conflicts yet remain," urging that they "dauntless keep the heav'nly road."

Pilgrim's Farewell exists in both a four-part (SATB) version and the three-part (TTB) version printed here. Most of the early sources, including *The Psalmodist's Companion,* give the four-part setting. The three-part setting was first published in Jeremiah Ingalls' *The Christian Harmony* (Exeter, N.H., 1805), where, however, it was printed with the text "Let us rise." The refrain—both the music and the text "I'll march to Canaan's land . . . And troubles come no more" (measures 14–22)—first appeared in the 1802 *Harmony of Harmony.* The earliest source to combine the three-part version (which subsequently became the standard one), all four stanzas of the text, and the revivalist refrain was John Wyeth's *Repository of Sacred Music, Part Second* (Harrisburg, 1813), where the piece is printed in G major, a step higher than in earlier sources. The present edition is based upon the version found in the second edition of *Part Second* (Harrisburg, 1820).

PILGRIM'S FAREWELL

For performance

    Part Second gives no indications of tempo, dynamics, or ornamentation. The editor has suggested a tempo somewhat quicker than the $\quarternote = 60$ recommended by E. K. Dare in his prefatory remarks to *Part Second*. *Pilgrim's Farewell* can be performed successfully by a large chorus, a chamber ensemble, or soloists. The editor has scored the upper parts (which the source gives in the treble clef) for tenors. However, both tenor parts may be sung by sopranos instead of tenors (as called for in the source), or tenors may be doubled by sopranos. If the tessituras of the individual parts seem uncomfortably high, the editor recommends singing *Pilgrim's Farewell* a whole step lower (in F major).

51
PILGRIM'S FAREWELL

For TTB and/or SSB a cappella

Anonymous   Anonymous

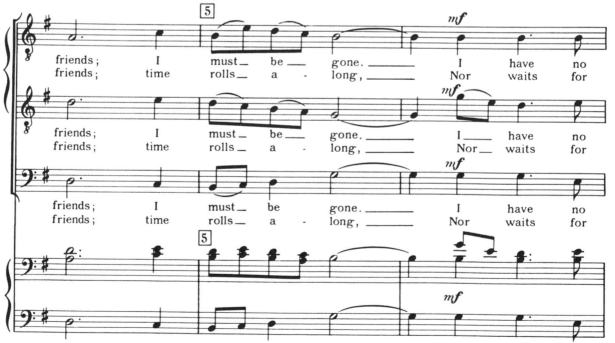

* If sopranos are used instead of tenors, the right hand should be played an octave higher.

** Original: **f♯**

REFRAIN

3. Farewell, dear brethren in the Lord;
   To you I'm bound with cords of love:
   But we believe his gracious word;
   We all ere long shall meet above.

Refrain: I'll march to .....

4. Farewell, ye blooming sons of God;
   Sore conflicts yet remain for you.
   But dauntless keep the heav'nly road,
   Till Canaan's happy land you view.

Refrain: I'll march to .....

Biographical Notes

Asahel Benham (1757–1805) was a native of New Hartford, Connecticut. He seems to have received little formal education, and, unlike most singing-masters, he appears to have followed no other profession or trade. His income was evidently derived entirely from the teaching of singing-schools: he was active in this calling throughout New England and the Middle Atlantic States. He eventually settled in Wallingford, Connecticut. Two important collections of sacred vocal music bear his name: the *Federal Harmony* (New Haven, 1790) and the *Social Harmony* (New Haven, 1798).

Although attribution of the *Redemption Anthem* cannot be made with certainty, surviving evidence would seem to indicate that the composer was Benham. Like other compilers of late eighteenth-century collections, Benham himself did not identify those pieces in his anthologies which other evidence now leads us to believe he composed. Thus, while Benham does not claim for himself any of the pieces in the six editions of the *Federal Harmony,* several of these compositions are attributed to him by fellow compilers, including the Connecticut tunesmith Oliver Brownson, a close associate of Benham's. The *Redemption Anthem* first appeared in the *Social Harmony,* where it bears no attribution. Of the 45 pieces in this collection, 36 are given attributions (Benham himself is not among the composers named), and two more carry the ascription "Unknown." On these grounds it may be inferred that the seven remaining compositions are actually Benham's. Moreover, William Walker in *The Southern Harmony* (New Haven, 1835), a tune-book of the Southern tradition, ascribes the *Redemption Anthem* to "Benham." (In Ananias Davisson's *Kentucky Harmony* [Harrisonburg, Virginia, c. 1815], however, it is attributed to the English psalmodist [Joseph] "Stephenson." No other evidence has been found to support the latter attribution.)

William Billings (1746–1800) was perhaps the most gifted composer to emerge from the New England singing-school tradition. A friend of such patriots as Samuel Adams and Paul Revere (who engraved some of his music), he was an ardent supporter of the American Revolution. Although by trade a tanner, he seems to have devoted most of his energy to composing music and teaching singing-schools, largely in the Boston area. Billings brought out six tune-books and a variety of smaller musical publications.

Lucius Chapin (1760–1842) was a native of Massachusetts. After serving as a fifer in the Revolutionary War, he settled for a while on Staten Island. In 1791, together with his wife Susan and brother Amzi, Chapin traveled to Virginia. In 1797, he moved westward, settling on the homestead known as "Vernon," near Washington, Kentucky. He and his brother were among the earliest singing-masters to conduct schools west of the Alleghenies. Their widespread reputation as musicians and teachers may account for the numerous attributions to "Chapin" in tune-books of the Southern tradition. However, recent research indicates that only four tunes (including *Rockbridge*) can be ascribed to Lucius with any certainty, while only three pieces can be assigned to Amzi.

Elkanah Kelsay Dare (1782–1826) was a Methodist clergyman, composer, and dean of boys at the now defunct Wilmington College in Wilmington, Delaware. Active when the New England singing-school tradition had begun to decline in the Northeast, Dare resisted the European style of religious music and staunchly defended the efforts of American composers. Dare appears to have played a prominent role in the musical organization of John Wyeth's *Repository of Sacred Music, Part Second* (Harrisburg, 1813). He also contributed to *Part Second* both the prefatory remarks on the rudiments of music and thirteen of his own compositions.

Horatio Garnet (fl. c. 1790) is known only by *An Ode for the Fourth of July,* published in the first volume of the *Massachusetts Magazine* (July, 1789) and reprinted in *The American Musical Miscellany* (Northampton, 1798). The traditional European style of this composition suggests that Garnet may have been one of the English composers who emigrated to New England in the late eighteenth century.

Oliver Holden (1765–1844) ranks among the most influential composer-compilers of the New England singing-school tradition. Born in Shirley, Massachusetts, he served during the Revolution as a marine; he later represented Charlestown, Massachusetts (where he had settled in 1787), in the Massachusetts House of Representatives. A Puritan minister, he supplemented his income by working at various times as a carpenter, music-store proprieter, and real-estate *entrepreneur.* Holden shared the view held by the Connecticut composer Andrew Law that the sacred works of Yankee tunesmiths were stylistically flawed and inferior to those of their European contemporaries. Advocating the adoption of the European style, he included works by European composers in his own collections. Moreover, he appears to have been one of the first American composers to have had grounding in traditional harmony. *The Massachusetts Compiler* (Boston, 1795), a collection which he edited in collaboration with Samuel Holyoke and Hans Gram, was one of the first tune-books to reflect European influence. In addition to this collection, Holden was responsible for at least eight other important tune-books.

Samuel Holyoke (1762–1820) was one of the most prolific composers of the New England singing-school tradition. Born at Boxford, Massachusetts, he composed his most popular tune, *Arnheim,* when only 16. After having been graduated from Harvard, Holyoke served as instructor at the Groton Academy (later the Lawrence Academy) from 1793 to 1800. In the latter year he settled in Salem, Massachusetts, from where he traveled to neighboring towns to conduct singing-schools and concerts. Like Oliver Holden, Holyoke appears to have had some knowledge of traditional harmony. He and Holden were associated with Hans Gram in the publication of *The Massachusetts Compiler* (Boston, 1795), a collection influenced by European styles. He edited or coedited at least eight other influential tune-books, one of them containing his own instrumental compositions, which are among the earliest instrumental music published in America. Holyoke became ill with "lung fever" while teaching singing-school in Concord, New Hampshire, and died there in February 1820.

BIOGRAPHICAL NOTES

Jeremiah Ingalls (1764–1838), like many other New England composers of his day, was a man of many occupations. For some years a tavern-keeper, he was also at various times a barrel-maker, a farmer, a singing-master, a choir director, and a Congregational deacon. Born in Andover, Massachusetts, he moved in 1791 to Newbury, Vermont. He played bass viol, sang, and, for specific occasions, composed pieces such as his *Election Ode* and *Lamentation,* the latter a memorial for the death of one Judith Brock, who died of lockjaw at the age of 19. Ingalls' tune-book, *The Christian Harmony* (Exeter, N.H., 1805), is one of the earliest printed collections to contain a substantial number of folk-hymns.

Walter Janes (1779–1827) was born at Ashford, Connecticut. A mason by trade, Janes was also a composer, singing-master, and poet. In 1825, Janes conducted the music at the ceremony for the laying of the corner-stone of the Bunker Hill monument in Charlestown, Massachusetts. He is known to have published only two collections, the *Massachusetts Harmony* (Boston, 1803) and the *Harmonic Minstrelsy* (Dedham, Mass., 1807).

Stephen Jenks (1771–1856) was a native of New Canaan, Connecticut. Active as a teacher, composer, and compiler of numerous tune-books, Jenks lived successively in Ridgefield and New Salem, Connecticut, and in Providence, Rhode Island. The father of eight children, he settled in 1829 in Thompson, Ohio, where he manufactured drums and tambourines until his death.

Andrew Law (1748–1821) was a native of Milford, Connecticut. He received an M.A. from Rhode Island College in 1778. He subsequently studied theology, was ordained at Hartford in 1787, and served as a Congregational minister in Philadelphia and Baltimore. Law devoted much of his energy to compiling tune-books, writing instructional manuals for singers and keyboard players, devising a system of shape notation, and conducting singing-schools. He strongly advocated musical reforms intended to introduce to Americans the "scientific" methods of European music.

Lewer is known only by the three-part piece *Fidelia,* the single composition attributed to him in *Wyeth's Repository of Sacred Music, Part Second* (Harrisburg, 1813).

Justin Morgan (1747–1798), by profession a school-master, was a self-taught musician who supplemented his meager income by operating a boatmen's tavern on the Connecticut River and by keeping thoroughbred stallions at stud. (A horse he owned until his death was the progenitor of the breed known as Morgan horses.) Seeking relief from tuberculosis, Morgan in 1788 moved his family to the more healthful climate of Randolf Center, a hill-town in Vermont. Despite his illness, Morgan taught singing-schools throughout central Vermont. Instructing children by day and adults at night, he traveled from town to town during the winters until his death in 1798. Although Morgan is said to have left a manuscript volume of music upon his death, only nine of his compositions have survived. Eight of these, including *Amanda* and the *Judgment Anthem,* were first published in Asahel Benham's *Federal Harmony* (New Haven, 1790).

BIOGRAPHICAL NOTES

Daniel Read (1757–1836) was born at Attleboro, Massachusetts. After serving as a private during the Revolution, Read settled in New Haven, becoming one of Connecticut's most influential composers. Like many singing-masters, he was a man of several occupations, among them general storekeeper and comb manufacturer. He was not only responsible for the publication of numerous tune-books between 1785 and 1810, but was also the founder of the first American musical periodical, *The American Musical Magazine* (1786–87). One of the most popular of all the New England singing-school composers, Read was especially prolific as a writer of fuging-tunes.

Robison. Nothing is known of this composer, for whom *Wyeth's Repository of Sacred Music, Part Second* (Harrisburg, 1813) provides attributions for two tunes; both of these are published in the present collection. In the first edition of *Part Second,* the composer's name is spelled "Robinson."

William Selby (1738–1798) was active in London as an organist and composer during the 1760s. In 1771 he emigrated to Boston, where he was appointed organist at King's Chapel (later renamed Stone Chapel). He held this position for most of the remainder of his life. In Boston he organized and conducted numerous concerts, frequently performing himself as organist and harpsichordist. He endeavored to publish secular vocal and instrumental compositions like those of his works engraved during his early London career; these efforts, however, were largely unsuccessful, perhaps because he was unable to overcome the stiff resistance to such music by pious Congregationalist Bostonians. He died in relative poverty on December 12, 1798.

P. Sherman. Almost nothing is known of this composer, who is represented in only two tune-books, both of which were issued after the New England singing-school tradition had begun to decline: Daniel Peck's *The Musical Medley* (Dedham, Mass., 1808) contains 18 pieces attributed to "P. Sherman," and the same compiler's *A Valuable Selection* (Philadelphia, 1810) includes 16 compositions assigned to "Sherman." Several Sherman tunes continued to be popular in the Southern tradition.

Elisha West (1756–after 1808). Little about West's early career has come down to us. He was married in Maine on December 1, 1776, and in 1791 settled in Woodstock, Vermont, where he earned his living as a farmer. West soon became the most influential musician in the Woodstock area, earned a reputation as a superior singer, and led numerous singing-schools during winters. He appears to have compiled only one tune-book, *The Musical Concert* (Northampton, 1802; 2nd edition, 1807).

J. West. Nothing is known of the career of this composer. The several attributions to him in Elisha West's *The Musical Concert* (Northampton, 1802) might suggest that the two men may have been related.

BIOGRAPHICAL NOTES

White. Nothing is known of this composer. Irving Lowens suggests (introduction to the facsimile edition of *Wyeth's Repository of Sacred Music, Part Second*, p. xiii) that White, who is represented by only one composition in *Part Second*, is probably the same man with whom Ananias Davisson collaborated in the composition of several pieces first printed in *The Supplement to the Kentucky Harmony* (Harrisonburg, Va., 1820).

Abraham Wood (1752–1804) was born in Northboro, Massachusetts, where he later married, fathered thirteen children, and operated his family's cloth manufacturing business. He left Northboro to serve in the Revolutionary War militia, first as a drummer for the Lexington Alarms in 1774, then as a soldier, and finally as the elected captain of a company. He was a member of a Committee of Correspondence in 1777 and 1780, and served as an Assessor of Towns in 1781–82, when the first municipal taxes were levied in the new State of Massachusetts. Wood published several tune-books and sang in the choir of the Congregational (now Unitarian) church in Northboro; his more than 40 published compositions were probably written for this choir.

Bibliography

The American Musical Miscellany (Northampton, 1798; reprint, Brooklyn, 1972).

Anderson, Gillian, editor. *The Christmas Music of William Billings* (Washington, D.C., 1973–   ).

———. *Political and Patriotic Music of the American Revolution* (Washington, D.C., 1973–   ).

Barbour, J. Murray. *The Church Music of William Billings* (East Lansing, 1960).

Beeman, Anna [compiler and editor]. *Hymns on Various Subjects* (Norwich, Conn., 1792).

Billings, William. *The Complete Works*, ed. by Hans Nathan, Richard Crawford, et. al., forthcoming.

Bourne, Hugh [compiler]. *A Collection of Hymns, for Camp Meetings, Revivals &c. For the Use of the Primitive Methodists* (Bemersley, near Tunstall, East Suffolk, 1829).

Britton, Allen P. "The Singing School Movement in the United States," *Report of the Eighth Congress of the International Musicological Society*, I (Papers) (Kassel, 1961), 89–99.

———. "Theoretical Introductions in American Tune-Books to 1800" (Ph.D. dissertation, University of Michigan, 1949).

Bronson, Bertrand. *The Ballad as Song* (Berkeley, 1969).

Buechner, Alan C. "Yankee Singing Schools and the Golden Age of Choral Music in New England, 1760–1800" (Ph.D. dissertation, Harvard University, 1960).

Butts, Thomas [compiler]. *Harmonia Sacra* (London, [1765?]).

The Camp-Meeting Chorister; or, a Collection of Hymns and Spiritual Songs for the Pious of All Denominations (Philadelphia, 1849).

Chapman, James G., editor. *Vermont Harmony: A Collection of Fuging Tunes, Anthems, and Secular Pieces by Vermont Composers of the Period 1790 to 1810 Including the Complete Works of Justin Morgan* (Burlington, 1972).

Chappell, William. *Old English Popular Music*. A new edition with a preface and notes, and the earlier examples entirely revised by H. Ellis Wooldridge. Supplement to *Chappell's Traditional Tunes*, collected & edited by F. Kidson. (New York, 1893).

Chase, Gilbert. *America's Music* (New York, 1955).

Cheney, Simeon Pease [editor]. *The American Singing Book* (Boston, 1879).

A Collection of Hymns For the Use of the Church of Christ, Meeting in Angel-Alley, Whitechapel, Margaret-Street, near Oxford-Market, and other Churches in Fellowship with Them (London, 1759).

BIBLIOGRAPHY

Crawford, Richard. *Andrew Law, American Psalmodist* (Evanston, 1968).

Crossman, Samuel. *The Young Man's Meditation, or Some Few Sacred Poems upon Select Subjects and Scriptures* (London, 1664).

Daniel, Ralph T. *The Anthem in New England before 1800* (Evanston, 1966).

Doddridge, Philip. *Hymns Founded on Various Texts in the Holy Scriptures, By the Late Philip Doddridge, D.D.* (London, 1755).

Dow, Lorenzo [compiler]. *A Collection of Spiritual Songs, Used at the Camp-Meetings, in the Great Revival, in the United States of America; A New Edition corrected* (Omagh, County Tyrone, 1829).

Echols, Paul C. Notes for the Western Wind recording *Early American Vocal Music,* Nonesuch H-71276 (New York, 1973).

Evans, Charles. *American Bibliography* (Worcester, Mass., 1903–59 and 1970 supplement).

Genuchi, Marvin C. "The Life and Music of Jacob French (1754–1817), Colonial American Composer" (Ph.D. dissertation, State University of Iowa, 1963).

Goldman, Richard Franko. *Landmarks of Early American Music, 1760–1800* (New York, 1943).

Green, Richard, compiler. *The Works of John and Charles Wesley: A Bibliography* (London, 1896).

Hamm, Charles. "The Chapins and Sacred Music in the South and West," *Journal of Research in Music Education,* VIII (1960), 91–98.

Held, Jerrold Frederic. "A Critical Analysis of the Music of an American Colonial Composer, Abraham Wood" (M.A. thesis, Rutgers University, 1963).

Hitchcock, H. Wiley. *Music in the United States: A Historical Introduction,* second edition (Englewood Cliffs, 1974).

———. "William Billings and the Yankee Tunesmiths," *Hi Fi/Stereo Review,* XVI (1966), 55–65.

Jackson, George Pullen, editor. *Another Sheaf of White Spirituals* (Gainesville, 1952).

———, editor. *Down-East Spirituals and Others* (Locust Valley, N.Y., 1939; reprint, New York, 1975).

———, editor. *Spiritual Folk-Songs of Early America* (Locust Valley, N.Y., 1937).

———. *White and Negro Spirituals* (Locust Valley, N.Y., 1943; reprint, New York, 1975).

———. *White Spirituals in the Southern Uplands* (Chapel Hill, 1933; reprint, New York, 1965).

Johnson, Allen, editor. *Dictionary of American Biography* (New York, 1928–36).

Johnson, Charles A. "Camp Meeting Hymnody," *American Quarterly,* IV (1952), 110–26.

———. "The Frontier Camp Meeting: Contemporary and Historical Appraisals, 1805–1840," *The Mississippi Valley Historical Review*, XXXVII (1950), 91–110.

———— . *The Frontier Camp Meeting, Religion's Harvest Time* (Dallas, 1955).

Julian, John. *A Dictionary of Hymnology*, second revised edition, with new supplement (London, 1907; reprint, New York, 1957).

Koler, Louise E. "Man Overshadowed by a Horse: Justin Morgan, Composer and Teacher," *News and Notes of the Vermont Historical Society*, VI (1955), 81–84.

Lindsley, Charles Edward. "Scoring and Placement of the 'Air' in Early American Tunebooks," *The Musical Quarterly*, LVIII (1972), 365–82.

Little, Thomas. *See* Thomas Moore.

Lowens, Irving. "Introduction" to the reprint of the fifth edition of *Wyeth's Repository of Sacred Music* (New York, 1974), vii–xviii.

———— . "Introduction" to the reprint of the second edition of *Wyeth's Repository of Sacred Music, Part Second* (New York, 1964), v–xvi.

———— . *Music and Musicians in Early America* (New York, 1964).

———— . "The Origins of the American Fuging Tune," *Journal of the American Musicological Society*, VI (1953), 43–52.

———— , and Allen P. Britton. "The Easy Instructor (1798–1831): A History and Bibliography of the First Shape Note Tune Book," *Journal of Research in Music Education*, I (1953), 31–55.

Madan, Martin [compiler]. *A Collection of Psalms and Hymns extracted from Various Authors* (London, 1760).

Marrocco, W. Thomas, and Harold Gleason, editors. *Music in America* (New York, 1964).

The Massachusetts Magazine, I (1789) and II (1790).

McCormick, David W. "Oliver Holden, Composer and Anthologist" (S.M.D. dissertation, Union Theological Seminary, 1963).

McCutchan, Robert. *Our Hymnody: A Manual of the Methodist Hymnal* (New York, 1937).

McKay, David P. "William Selby, Musical Emigré in Colonial Boston," *The Musical Quarterly*, LVII (1971), 609–27.

———— , and Richard Crawford. "The Performance of William Billings' Music," *Journal of Research in Music Education*, XXI (1973), 318–30.

———— . *William Billings of Boston* (Princeton, 1975).

Metcalf, Frank J. *American Writers and Compilers of Sacred Music* (New York, 1925; reprint, New York, 1967).

Moore, Thomas. *The Poetical Works of Thomas Moore, Collected by Himself*, 10 vols. (London, 1840–41; first American edition, New York, 1853).

———— [Thomas Little]. *The Poetical Works of the Late Thomas Little, Esq.* (Philadelphia, 1804).

Murray, Sterling E. "Performance Practice in Early American Psalmody," to appear in *The American Choral Review*.

BIBLIOGRAPHY

———— . "Timothy Swan and Yankee Psalmody," *The Musical Quarterly,* LXI (1975), 433–63.

Nathan, Hans. "Billings, William," *Die Musik in Geschichte und Gegenwart,* XV (Kassel, 1973), cols. 798–99.

———— . "William Billings: A Bibliography," *Notes,* XXIX (1973), 658–69.

Occom, Samson. *A Choice Collection of Hymns and Spiritual Songs* (New London, Conn., 1774).

Patterson, Relford. "Three American 'Primitives': A Study of the Musical Styles of Samuel Holyoke, Oliver Holden, and Hans Gram" (Ph.D. dissertation, Washington University, 1963).

Pope, Alexander. *The Poems of Alexander Pope* (The Twickenham Edition), edited by John Butt et al. (London, 1939–69).

Pratt, Waldo Selden, editor. *Grove's Dictionary of Music and Musicians, American Supplement* to the third edition (New York, 1928).

Rippon, John. *A Selection of Hymns from the Best Authors* (London, 1878; first American edition, New York, 1792).

Roscommon, Wentworth Dillon, 4th Earl of. *Poetical Works* (Edinburgh, 1793).

Scholten, James W. "Amzi Chapin: Frontier Singing Master and Folk Hymn Composer," *Journal of Research in Music Education,* XXIII (1975), 109–19.

———— . "The Chapins: A Study of Men and Sacred Music West of the Alleghenies, 1795–1842" (Ed.D. dissertation, University of Michigan, 1972).

Shaw, Ralph R., and Richard H. Shoemaker. *American Bibliography: A Preliminary Checklist for 1801–1819* (New York, 1958–63).

Shipton, Clifford K., and James E. Mooney. *National Index of American Imprints through 1800; The Short-title Evans* (Barre, Mass., 1969).

Slonimsky, Nicolas. *Baker's Biographical Dictionary of Musicians,* fifth edition (New York, 1958) and Supplement (New York, 1971).

Smith, Joshua. *Divine Hymns, or Spiritual Songs,* eighth Exeter edition (Exeter, N.H., 1801).

Sonneck, Oscar G. *A Bibliography of Early Secular American Music,* revised & enlarged edition by William T. Upton (Washington, D.C., 1945; reprint, New York, 1964).

———— . *Early Concert-Life in America (1731–1800)* (Leipzig, 1907; reprint, New York, 1949).

Stephen, Sir Leslie, and Sir Sidney Lee. *Dictionary of National Biography* (London, 1917–   ).

Stevenson, Robert. *Protestant Church Music in America* (New York, 1966).

Tate, Nahum, and Nicholas Brady. *A New Version of the Psalms of David* (London, 1696).

Walter, Thomas. *The Grounds and Rules of Musick Explained: Or, An Introduction to the Art of Singing by Note* (Boston, 1721).

BIBLIOGRAPHY

Watts, Isaac. *Horae Lyricae* (London, 1706; first American edition, Philadelphia, 1741).

————. *Hymns and Spiritual Songs* (London, 1707; first American edition, Boston, *ca.* 1720).

————. *The Psalms of David, Imitated in the Language of the New Testament* (London, 1719; first American edition, Philadelphia, 1729).

White, B. F., and E. J. King. *The Sacred Harp,* reprint of the third edition (Philadelphia, 1859) with historical introduction, *The Story of the Sacred Harp 1844–1944,* by G. P. Jackson (Nashville, 1968).

Wilhide, J. Laurence. "Samuel Holyoke: American Music Educator" (Ph.D. dissertation, University of Southern California, 1954).

Indexes

Voicings

Numbers are the serial numbers assigned to pieces in *The Western Wind American Tune-Book*. Only the voicings designated by the editor in the present edition are listed here; other alternatives and doublings are suggested in the Introduction.

SB	33, 35, 36, 38
TB	28, 32, 34, 39
SSB	12, 37
STB	1
ATB	24
TTB	4, 21, 26, 27, 40, 41, 42, 47, 49, 51
SATB	2, 3, 5, 6, 7, 8, 9, 10, 11, 13, 14, 15, 16, 17, 18, 19, 20, 22, 23, 25, 29, 30, 31, 44, 46, 48, 50
STTB	45
SATB (double chorus)	43

Sources

Tune-Books on Which the Present Editions Are Based

Numbers are the serial numbers assigned to pieces in *The Western Wind American Tune-Book.* Pieces are entered under a specific tune-book only if the editor has used the version in that tune-book as the principal source of his edition of the piece.

American Harmony (Boston, 1792), 1, 17, 46

The American Singing-Book (New Haven, 1785), 18, 30, 44

The Christian Harmony (Exeter, N.H., 1805), 2, 8, 26, 27, 41, 42

The Columbian Harmonist No. 3 (New Haven, 1795), 48

The Columbian Harmony (Boston, 1793), 20

*The Continental Harmony** (Boston, 1794), 9, 10, 50

The Delights of Harmony (Dedham, Mass., 1805), 7, 12, 14

The Evangelical Harmony (Boston, 1800), 19

Federal Harmony (New Haven, 1790), 29

Harmonic Minstrelsy (Dedham, Mass., 1807), 16

The Harmony of Zion (Dedham, Mass., 1818), 13

The Massachusetts Compiler (Boston, 1795), 24

The Massachusetts Magazine (1789–90), 47, 49

The Musical Concert (Northampton, 1802), 6

The Musical Medley (Dedham, Mass., 1808), 31

*The Singing-Master's Assistant** (Boston, 1778), 11

The Union Harmony (Boston, 1793), 5

*Wyeth's Repository of Sacred Music, Part Second,** second edition (Harrisburg, 1820), 3, 4, 21, 22, 23, 25, 28, 32, 33, 34, 35, 36, 37, 38, 39, 40, 43, 45, 51

---

*Available in facsimile edition.

Titles

Numbers are the serial numbers assigned to pieces in *The Western Wind American Tune-Book.*

First Lines

Numbers are the serial numbers assigned to pieces in *The Western Wind American Tune-Book.*

INDEX OF FIRST LINES

Poets

Numbers are the serial numbers assigned to pieces in *The Western Wind American Tune-Book.*

Anonymous, 6, 7, 12, 13, 19, 22, 25, 26, 27, 32, 33, 39, 40, 43, 49, 51
Bible, 9, 10, 11, 50
Billings, William, 50
Cennick, John, 24, 25
Crossman, Samuel, 51
Doddridge, Philip, 3, 35
George, Daniel, 47
Hibard, Elder, 41
Leland, John, 8, 42
Madan, Martin, 24
Moore, Thomas, 12
Niles, Nathaniel, 15
Pope, Alexander, 1
Rippon, John, 24
Robinson, Robert, 34, 36
Roscommon, Wentworth Dillon, 4th Earl of, 50
Stennett, 14
Tate, Nahum, 44
Tate, Nahum, and Nicholas Brady, 23
Watts, Isaac, 2, 4, 5, 16, 17, 18, 20, 21, 25, 28, 29, 30, 31, 37, 38, 46, 48
Wesley, Charles, 24, 25, 45

Composers

Numbers are the serial numbers assigned to pieces in *The Western Wind American Tune-Book*.

Anonymous, 3, 4, 23, 32, 33, 34, 36, 39, 40, 51
Benham, Asahel, 43
Billings, William, 9, 10, 11, 50
Chapin, Lucius, 37
Dare, Elkanah Kelsay, 22, 45
Garnet, Horatio, 49
Holden, Oliver, 1, 5, 17, 46
Holyoke, Samuel, 24
Ingalls, Jeremiah, 2, 26, 27, 41, 42
Janes, Walter, 16
Jenks, Stephen, 7, 12, 13, 14
Law, Andrew, 15
Lewer, 21
Morgan, Justin, 25, 29
Read, Daniel, 18, 30, 44, 48
Robison, 35, 38
Selby, William, 47
Sherman, P., 31
West, Elisha, 8
West, J., 6
White, 28
Wood, Abraham, 19, 20